Also available…

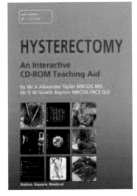

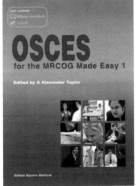

A Guide to the Part 2 MRCOG Examination

Author
Mr S John Duthie MBChB FRCOG
Consultant Obstetrician & Gynaecologist
Blackpool Fylde and Wyre Hospitals NHS Foundation Trust

Published by Dalton Square Medical Ltd

Dalton Square Medical Ltd a company registered in England and Wales under number 6572579 and whose registered office is at PO Box 6587, Bournemouth, Dorset, BH4 0BL

Edited by A Alexander Taylor

First published 2009

ISBN 978-0-9555690-3-6

British Library Cataloguing in Publication Data
A catalogue record for this book is available from the British Library

Library of Congress Cataloguing in Publication Data
A catalogue record for this book is available from the Library of Congress

Note
Medical knowledge is constantly changing. As new information becomes available, changes in treatment, procedures, equipment and the use of drugs become necessary. The editor, contributors and the publishers have, as far as it is possible, taken care to ensure that the information given in this text is accurate and up to date. However, readers are strongly advised to confirm that the information, especially with regard to drug usage, complies with the latest legislation and standards of practice.

Printed in England by Colin Cross Printers 01995 604368

Contents

Foreword

The Part 2 MRCOG examination is one of the more difficult postgraduate examinations in the United Kingdom and can appear very daunting to a prospective candidate. Candidates sometimes, don't know where to start and where to end. When I started my preparation for the exam I was told by Dr Tom McFarlane Consultant Obstetrician and Gynaecologist that "a large part of the exam tests clinical experience and technique".

There is a missing link or a gap between the MRCOG exam and the available textbooks. This gap is amplified as the exam is based on UK practice and yet most of the candidates are from overseas. Not all these candidates, will have had the opportunity to be exposed to the highly organised NHS maternity services.

A friend suggested that I have a look at mrcogadvantage.com and for OSCEs, to look at the DVDs "OSCES for the MRCOG made easy Volume 1 & 2"; I was initially reluctant to download more essay questions and add it to the pile of papers I had. At the first reading of the questions I found some were extremely easy and the others were so difficult.

Then I started to answer some of the questions and I started to feel low as I answered the easy ones badly in comparison to the model-scoring sheet. Then I started to read the scoring answer sheet and the model answer. I found by comparing the scoring sheet and the model answer that I gained an insight into what the examiner wanted. It taught me how to improve my writing technique, in a well-organised way in order to score. It also taught me how to think and tackle difficult questions even if I did not have the sufficient background experience. The more I read these questions the more confident I felt in tackling and answering any question in an organised and meticulous way. These questions bought the pieces of the puzzle together; I learnt the technique was important than raw knowledge.

I also went through the EMQ questions; they were so difficult and they demonstrated that the MRCOG has no knowledge limits. There are a lot of facts, which I had to "Google", as the answers were difficult to find in textbooks. But it gave me an insight into intelligent guessing.

I believe this book is invaluable in that it provides:-
- Guidance to the candidates about how the exam is structured.
- How to prepare for the exam.
- References to RCOG guidelines and important recent articles and how to access them.
  (more or less, it is a mini-syllabus to the exam).
- All the Short Answer Questions (SAQs) which have ever been set, which I think personally are very important. The study of past papers helps you get oriented and develop the "feel" of real exam questions. It gives you the confidence to tackle SAQs, some of the answers to which are on the trainees' website at the RCOG. These questions also help you to get an idea of the trend of exam questions and what topics you should concentrate more on; especially if they haven't appeared in the last two years.
- Advice on how to tackle EMQs and what is expected from you as a candidate
- Two OSCE worked examples; which highlight the structure of the exam.

The mrcogadvantage.com website and this guide are extremely helpful for a candidate preparing for the exam. Both were developed with a focus on delivering examination success, by an author who is a Consultant in the Speciality with inside experience and knowledge of the RCOG examination rules and regulations.

Mr Osama Soltan
MBBCh, DFFP, MRCOG
Specialist Trainee

Introduction

One of the spurs to writing "A Guide to the Part 2 MRCOG Examination", was the release of The MRCOG: A Guide to the Examination published by the Royal College Press in 2008. This is the "official version", with useful information and some hints and tips. Perhaps a useful analogy in placing these two in context with each other would be to view "The MRCOG: A Guide to the Examination" as the official brochure of, say, the country's national tourist board and "A Guide to the Part 2 MRCOG Examination" as an unofficial but in-depth "Rough Guide" or "Lonely Planet" type guidebook.

S J Duthie

Acknowledgement

I would like to acknowledge Dr Paul D Hodges who gave me an invaluable amount of help in preparing this book. Dr Hodges is Deputy to the Head of the Examinations Department of the Royal College of Obstetricians and Gynaecologists. Among his many tasks, he expertly contributes to the assembly of the actual papers for the Part 1 and Part 2 MRCOG examinations.

Dr Hodges is a graduate of York University where he obtained a Bachelor of Arts degree in History. Subsequently, he wrote a thesis on Military History and obtained a Doctorate from the Birbeck University in London. Dr Hodges is an expert in blueprinting and standard setting techniques having published extensively in those areas. Dr Hodges and I have co-authored 2 books on Extended Matching Questions for the Part 1 and Part 2 MRCOG examinations. His familiarity with all the components of the examination, makes his contribution to the book and website unique and invaluable.

About the author

John Duthie is a Consultant Obstetrician and Gynaecologist at the Blackpool, Fylde and Wyre Hospitals NHS Trust. He graduated in medicine at Liverpool University and took up a Lectureship in Obstetrics and Gynaecology at the University of Hong Kong, followed by posts as Senior Registrar in Liverpool and Chester. He was appointed a full-time consultant in 1995. For many years he has been passionate about medical education; he was appointed as an examiner for the DRCOG in 1997 and for the MRCOG in 2001. He served on the Part 2 EMQ committee as a founding member from its inception in 2003 to 2006. He has taught on several of the MRCOG revision courses and was co-convener of the official Royal College Part 2 Revision Course from 2005 to 2008. In March 2007 he was sponsored by the College to visit and liaise with the National Board of Medical Examiners in Philadelphia, USA on item development and assessment of test validity. This is his fourth textbook; previous texts, including two covering MRCOG EMQs have been bestsellers and well-reviewed and he has many publications in peer-reviewed journals. He is a founding member of the new RCOG Assessment Committee.

Basics

The Part 2 MRCOG is an international examination based in the United Kingdom intended to test core knowledge and experience in Obstetrics and Gynaecology. The MRCOG appears to be consolidating its status and recognition as the "gold standard" international examination for specialists in Obstetrics and Gynaecology. Its growth is continuing apace - particularly in Northern Africa, Pakistan and Eastern Europe. It is based on good current practice in the UK, though does not include specifics of, for example, UK law. Having said that, it will test knowledge of specific UK guidelines (those written by the Royal College of Obstetricians and Gynaecologists and those written by the National Institute of Clinical Excellence).

The Part 2 MRCOG examination has four different question formats.
*   The MCQ Paper mainly tests factual knowledge of Obstetrics and Gynaecology and related disciplines.
*   The EMQ Paper tests factual knowledge and clinical judgement in obstetrics and gynaecology and related disciplines.
*   The SAQ Papers tests clinical knowledge and experience with an emphasis on the ability to comment critically on topical issues.
*   The Oral Assessment, tests not only clinical knowledge but also clinical and professional skills and attitudes, especially effective communication.

The current timetable for the written Examination is;

EMQ & MCQ Papers	2 hr 45 mins
Lunch Break	45 mins
SAQ Paper 1 (4 questions)	1 hr 45 mins
Break	15 mins
SAQ Paper 2 (4 questions)	1 hr 45 mins

The oral assessment takes three hours.

The current distribution of marks within the written paper and the Royal College's recommendation for timing are as follows;

Short Answer Questions (8 in total):
60% of marks   26¼ minutes per question
Multiple Choice Questions (225):
25% of marks   c 24 seconds each
Extended Matching Questions (40):
15% of marks   c 112 seconds each

The written pass mark tends to be in the region of 56% to 61% but does vary due to standard setting. The pass rate also varies and is normally between 20% and 25% of all the candidates who take the examination.

Using the mrcogadvantage.com website & Dalton Square Medical Resources

What is the best way to prepare for the Part 2 written papers and oral assessment and how can the mrcogadvantage.com website help?
The answer will vary from candidate to candidate but I have made some notes which I hope you will find helpful. The two most significant questions for you to answer to yourself are as follows;

1. Am I ready to take the examination? If the answer is "yes" then this means that you have had the necessary depth of experience, gained the appropriate knowledge and had time to reflect on various modern concepts in Obstetrics and Gynaecology.
2. Have I enough time to prepare for the Part 2 MRCOG examination? The time needed to prepare will depend on various issues. However, it would be wise to allow six months to revise for a first attempt at the papers and at least three months for a second or subsequent attempt. In this context, it is worth noting that the website offers five complete sets of papers for enrolled clients. This means that someone obtaining all 40 SAQs would need 18 hours simply to write all the answers! Then, you will need to look at the model answers and (in most cases) do some reading. Someone obtaining all five EMQ papers would need about six hours to answer all of the material. These SAQs and EMQs will give you a wide experience in practising these papers. Some MCQ practice is also recommended – although they are more knowledge based and a far less challenging format that either the SAQ or EMQ formats – which is why the focus of the website is on SAQs and EMQs. It is intended that more SAQ and EMQ papers will be released soon. Please give yourself enough time.

Using the website should be easy enough. It has been designed to use standard internet protocols and to be as straightforward as possible – reflecting my own low level of technical prowess! If you hit any problems email mrcogadvantage@gmail.com for assistance.

Recommending "outside" reading for the Part 2 MRCOG is not an exact science. Good preparation should include a range of sources - not just one! Perhaps the most useful "short" book which is currently available would be; Obstetrics and Gynaecology - an evidence-based text for MRCOG, by David Luesley and Philip Baker. The new edition of Dewhurst's Textbook of Obstetrics and Gynaecology (7th edition) has been released. It is an authoritative textbook, up-to-date to 2007/8 and as such would be the core recommendation. The series of books in 'MRCOG and beyond' are excellent in terms of good value and focused revision of distinct areas which would be covered in Part 2 MRCOG. Most of the other larger textbooks should be regarded mainly as reference texts and referred to in libraries.

One of the best ways of preparing for the Part 2 MRCOG OSCEs is to watch, OSCEs for the MRCOG Made Easy Volume 1 & 2 (this second volume will be published at the same time as this revision aid). These provide gold standard filmed OSCEs for the first time, with a particular focus on communication issues and tips on how to maximize your communication skills.

SHORT ANSWER QUESTIONS

S
A
Q

The short answer questions (SAQs) account for 60% of the marks for the written paper. As such, they remain the single most important component of the written paper. The multiple choice questions account for 25% of the marks and the extended matching questions for 15%.

The main guidance for answering the short answer (previously known as essay) questions is to carefully read the questions and cover the questions evenly - keep an eye on the time. Many questions now provide guidance on the marking split, which should be followed carefully. There is no point repeating knowledge as it will only be rewarded once. Some additional sample short answer questions and answers – unfortunately now rather dated - are available in the trainees' section of the RCOG website at http://www.rcog.org.uk/index. asp?PageID=454

One of the most useful things which a candidate might find helpful is to consider the Examiner's mindset. What is the purpose of a question? Consider this example – 'How may the perinatal mortality rate be reduced further?' This is NOT an invitation to list 12 causes of perinatal mortality. Rather, it is a test to see whether you are a) aware of current challenges in Obstetrics b) someone who has thought further, rather than simply memorising the causes of perinatal loss and c) able to express your thoughts in a clear and logical manner.

The purpose of the Part 2 MRCOG examination is to be a valid test. What does this mean? A test is valid when it measures what it claims to measure and reliable when it does so consistently. This is an over-simplification, but what the examination candidate needs to know is that the examination is designed to measure the knowledge, attitude and skills of a year 5 Specialist Trainee in Obstetrics and Gynaecology. Therefore, the items that will come up in the written paper cover what you should know and be familiar with. It might help you to prepare if you think about what it is YOU need to know.

The examination covers breadth as well as the appropriate depth of knowledge. Consider this example – 'Discuss methods of control of pain in a woman with terminal gynaecological cancer.'
The answer should include the importance of prevention of pain as

5

well as the regular use of morphine based products to quell pain. The relief of established pain is more difficult and therefore analgesia must be used regularly. You need to discuss how oral drugs are more difficult to give if the woman has nausea. A lower dose of morphine can be administered by the subcutaneous route when compared with the oral route in order to achieve the same degree of analgesia. Your answer needs to cover breakthrough pain. So far, the answer shows that you are familiar with some of the aspects of pain relief in the example provided. How about covering other aspects? The use of antibiotics to control secondary infection is an important aspect of pain relief and deserves a place in your answer.

Consider another example – 'Discuss the maternal morbidity which may arise due to placenta praevia.' Most candidates would describe the risk of obstetric haemorrhage, DVT, renal failure, caesarean section and anaesthetic hazards. The good candidate would cover breadth as well as depth; massive bleeding could lead to cerebral hypoxia and death. Prolonged hypotension could lead to adult respiratory distress syndrome. Relatively fewer candidates would write about the long term and short term psychological morbidity which often arises following emergency hysterectomy.

The examples which I have provided cover a wide range of topics. Remember that the time allowed for each SAQ is 26 minutes. If you decide to obtain the papers for practising, allow yourself an adequate period of time to write the answers. I recommend that you choose a time when you are not on call and can be left undisturbed. Time yourself carefully. Avoid looking at books or references. There will be time for that later. Practise under examination conditions.

How can your time be utilised effectively? Read the SAQ. Underline the key words. Ask yourself; "Do I really understand the question?" Candidates have mistaken recto vaginal fistula for vesico vaginal fistula and vice versa. Candidates have mistaken small for dates for large for dates and vice versa. The next step is to plan your answer. Of the 26 minutes, spend at least two or three minutes planning your answer in a logical manner. From March 2006, the format of the SAQs changed; each question is divided into a number of parts and each part carries a certain number of marks which are clearly displayed. Consider this example:

'A woman presents with light vaginal bleeding at 37 weeks. The woman has a history of two previous caesarean sections. An earlier ultrasound suggests the placenta is anterior and low.

A. Describe how your initial assessment would help you to establish the correct diagnosis: (10marks)
B. Justify what investigations will be useful in her further management: (7 marks).
C. What specific intraoperative complications should this woman be advised about before undergoing caesarean section? (3 marks)

If you are planning the answer to this question you would be well advised to give half your time and attention to the first part of the SAQ which is worth 10 out of 20 marks. The third part of the SAQ is a straightforward question. The answer? Haemorrhage to the point of needing a blood transfusion, risk of caesarean hysterectomy, risk of injury to the bladder.

Once you have planned your answer, write the answer in prose. Lists are best avoided unless you are seriously running out of time. One of the main challenges faced by candidates, which practice will improve, is the need to write quickly but legibly.

Candidates often have trouble in starting the answer to a SAQ. This requires practise and knowledge of the subject. DO use an opening sentence that is relevant to the SAQ and maximises your marks. Consider this example;
'A 38-year-old woman who has been pregnant three times and has three living children, complains of an eight month history of amenorrhoea. Explain what you would look for on examination (10 marks) and justify the investigations you would request: (10 marks)'
A relevant opening would be;
I would assess the woman's general condition and look for facial erythaema, Cushingoid appearance, features of virilism, exopthalmos, fine tremor, features of anxiety, clubbing of the fingers and alopecia. I would measure her pulse rate and blood pressure, as sinus bradycardia is a sign of hypothyroidism. Sinus tachycardia may indicate hyperthyroidism and hypertension is a feature of Cushing syndrome.

DO NOT patronise or try and educate the examiner by stating the obvious; "Amenorrhoea is very significant and this woman must be looked at carefully".
The person marking the SAQs is fully aware of all this! You lose valuable time by writing irrelevant material.

Sometimes candidates experience difficulty in understanding what is meant by certain terms. "Justify" means that you must write about WHY you would recommend a certain course of action. "Explain" means that you must make something CLEAR by describing the relevant issues in more detail and by REVEALING RELEVANT FACTS. "Discuss" means that you are asked to write about the subject IN DETAIL TAKING INTO ACCOUNT A RANGE OF OPINION. "Debate" is an invitation to SUMMARISE THE POINTS FOR AND AGAINST AND TO END WITH YOUR CONCLUSION.

Candidates sometimes have trouble with the term "Counsel". This has three components; To DEFINE, EXPLORE and CLARIFY.

Check your answer. It is not advisable to keep coming back to cross out and rewrite segments of your work. However, you may find that you have missed something out and there would be an opportunity to amplify a point or express an opinion clearly. It is very important to demonstrate your knowledge to the examiner. Consider this SAQ;

A 20 year old woman is 12 weeks into her first pregnancy and books for antenatal care. Her serum tests positive for antibodies to hepatitis C virus (HCV). Outline the maternal (4 marks) and fetal (4 marks) implications. Explain the salient points of her antenatal care (12 marks).

One of the points of this woman's antenatal care is to write to a Paediatrician. Why? Your Examiner is interested to know whether you understand the relevance of the serological findings to antenatal, leading onto perinatal care. One way to write this part of the answer is as follows; I would write to the Paediatric team and inform them of the forthcoming confinement and ensure follow up of the baby. Antibodies to HCV would cross the placenta and the newborn's serum would test positive for several months. Therefore, repeat testing of the newborn is necessary in order to distinguish between perinatal infection and transplacental passage of antibody.

It is not enough simply to state that you would "involve the Paediatrician". Similarly, it is relevant to arrange consultation with a Gastroenterologist for review during pregnancy and LONG TERM care. While checking your answer you may find an area where further explanation would be useful.

Once you have checked your answer, move on. It is imperative that you complete all four SAQs in each paper. There is simply no point in answering three SAQs and not attempting the fourth – too many marks will be lost this way even if your three answers score highly.

The technique that I strongly recommend could be summarised as follows;
Read the SAQ and grasp the allocation of marks
Underline the key words
Plan your answer
Write your answer clearly
Check your answer
Move on

Once again, give yourself adequate time for preparation.

Question spotting – 'hot topics'

I am not totally happy offering advice on question spotting, as it is not always productive. It seems to be a particular obsession on a number of the candidates' forums. Their hit / success rate is not generally high. However, preparing for 'hot topics' does have some value as the committee to some extent, does like to cover the more recent and up-to-date guidelines compared to the older ones. Therefore, more recent guidelines are more likely to appear in SAQ papers and worth extra attention. Having said that, as blueprinting of the exam is done up to 10 months ahead of the exam date and question preparation can take a serious amount of time, really recently published guidelines are unlikely to be used as a source for examination items in the imminent test. Here is a list of 2007-8 guidelines that may be considered 'quite warm' topics if not exactly 'hot' topics with links to their free downloadable versions (PDF format):

Maternity Dashboard - Clinical Performance and Governance Score Card, Good Practice No 7, January 2008:
http://www.rcog.org.uk/resources/Public/pdf/goodpractice7MaternityDashboard.pdf

The Role of Emergency and Elective Interventional Radiology in Postpartum Haemorrhage, Good Practice No 6, June 2007
http://www.rcog.org.uk/resources/Public/pdf/goodpractice6a.pdf

Birth After Previous Caesarean Birth, Green-top No 45, February 2007
http://www.rcog.org.uk/resources/Public/pdf/green_top45_birthafter.pdf

Blood Transfusions in Obstetrics, Green-top No 47, December 2007
http://www.rcog.org.uk/resources/Public/pdf/Greentop47BloodTransfusions1207.pdf

Chickenpox in Pregnancy, Green-top No 13, September 2007
http://www.rcog.org.uk/resources/Public/pdf/greentop13_chickenpox0907.pdf

Management of Genital Herpes in Pregnancy, Green-top No 30, September 2007
http://www.rcog.org.uk/resources/Public/pdf/greentop30_genital_herpes0907.pdf

Long-Term Consequences of Polycystic Ovary Syndrome, Green-top No 33, December 2007
http://www.rcog.org.uk/resources/Public/pdf/green_top33_pcos_a.pdf

The Management of Post Hysterectomy Vaginal Vault Prolapse, Green-top No 46, October 2007
http://www.rcog.org.uk/resources/Public/pdf/green_top_46_posthysterectomy.pdf

Management of Premenstrual Syndrome, Green-top No 48, December 2007
http://www.rcog.org.uk/resources/Public/pdf/green_top48_pms.pdf

The Management of Third- and Fourth-Degree Perineal Tears, Green-top No 29, March 2007
http://www.rcog.org.uk/resources/Public/pdf/green_top29_management_third_a.pdf

Preventing Entry-related Gynaecological Laparoscopic Injuries, Green-top No 49, May 2008
http://www.rcog.org.uk/resources/Public/pdf/green_top49_
PreventingLaparoscopicInjury.pdf

Thromboembolic Disease in Pregnancy and the Puerperium: Acute Management, Green-top No 28, February 2007
http://www.rcog.org.uk/resources/Public/pdf/green_top_28_thromboembolic_
minorrevision.pdf

Umbilical Cord Prolapse, Green-top No 50, April 2008
http://www.rcog.org.uk/resources/Public/pdf/Greentop50UmbilicalCordProlapse.pdf

Hormone Replacement Therapy, NHS Choices, 2008
http://www.nhs.uk/conditions/Hormone-replacement-therapy/Pages/
Introduction.aspx?url=Pages/What-is-it.aspx

The changing Role of the gynaecologist in the management of women with cancer, Scientific Advisory Committee Opinion Paper 10, November 2007
http://www.rcog.org.uk/resources/Public/pdf/ChangingRoleSAC101207.pdf

Intrauterine infection and perinatal brain injury, Scientific Advisory Committee Opinion Paper 3, October 2007
http://www.rcog.org.uk/resources/Public/pdf/intrauterine_infection_sac3_1007.pdf

Perinatal Risks Associated with IVF, Scientific Advisory Committee Opinion Paper 8, February 2007
http://www.rcog.org.uk/resources/Public/pdf/perinatal_risk_sac80207.pdf

Vaccination against cervical cancer, Scientific Advisory Committee Opinion Paper 9, February 2007
http://www.rcog.org.uk/resources/Public/pdf/vaccination_cervical_cancersac9a0207.pdf

Home Births, RCOG and Royal College of Midwives Joint Statement No 2, April 2007
http://www.rcog.org.uk/resources/Public/pdf/home_births_rcog_rcm0607.pdf

Obesity and Reproductive Health – 53rd study group statement, 2007
http://www.rcog.org.uk/resources/public/pdf/study_gp_obesity.pdf

Renal Disease in Pregnancy, 54th Study Group statement, 2008
http://www.rcog.org.uk/resources/public/pdf/
RenalDiseaseStudyGroupConsensusViews.pdf

Teenage Pregnancy and Reproductive Health, 52nd Study Group statement, 2007
http://www.rcog.org.uk/resources/public/pdf/study_gp_teenagepregnancy.pdf

Management of sexual and reproductive health of people living with HIV infection, BHIVA, 2008
http://www.bhiva.org/files/file1030950.pdf

Management of HIV infection in pregnant women, BHIVA, 2008
http://www.bhiva.org/files/file1030945.pdf

Antenatal and postnatal mental health: clinical management and service guidance, NICE Clinical guideline No 45, February 2007
http://www.nice.org.uk/nicemedia/pdf/CG45fullguideline.pdf

Antenatal care: routine care for the healthy pregnant woman, NICE Clinical guideline No 62, March 2008
http://www.nice.org.uk/nicemedia/pdf/CG062NICEguideline.pdf

Diabetes in pregnancy: management of diabetes and its complications from pre-conception to the postnatal period, NICE Clinical guideline No 63, March 2008
http://www.nice.org.uk/nicemedia/pdf/CG063Guidance.pdf

Heavy menstrual bleeding: investigation and treatment, NICE Clinical guideline No 44, January 2007
http://www.nice.org.uk/nicemedia/pdf/CG44FullGuideline.pdf

Intrapartum care: management and delivery of care to women in labour, NICE Clinical guideline No 55, September 2007
http://www.nice.org.uk/nicemedia/pdf/IPCNICEGuidance.pdf

Mesh sacrocolpopexy for vaginal vault prolapse, NICE Interventional Procedure Guidance No 215, March 2007
http://www.nice.org.uk/nicemedia/pdf/IPG215guidance.pdf

Fetal cystoscopy for diagnosis and treatment of lower urinary outflow tract obstruction, Interventional Procedure Guidance No 205, January 2007
http://www.nice.org.uk/nicemedia/pdf/IPG205guidance.pdf

Question spotting – 'due topics'

I'm even more cautious in this area, trying to second-guess the SAQ committee is a risky business. Questions are not repeated that frequently, are often substantially revised when they are repeated and you should expect the majority of the eight questions to be brand new. Candidate forums do indulge in a lot of anticipating "due topics" – mainly as failing candidates get feedback with the full questions sent out to them, so the topics are 'out there'. With this proviso and caution underlined, to save you hard work scraping around the internet, I am pleased to summarise all (!) the SAQ question topics ever asked and the full questions of the last three 2007-8 sittings:

Essay topics September 1997 – March 2007 – Paper 1

	Q1	Q2	Q3	Q4	Q5
Sept 1997	Haemophilia A father pre-conception counselling	Debate need for antenatal beds in obs. unit	Advice pre-pregnancy having undergone a renal transplant	Treatments available to manage severe pre-eclampsia at 32 weeks	Advice when US shows a pregnancy in one horn of a bicornuate uterus (8 weeks with uterine bleeding)
March 1998	Advise request for induction at 40 weeks for 'personal reasons'	Consider place of vaginal delivery when only child delivered by caesarean	Appraise use of forceps in prolonged second stage due to occipito-posterior fetal head at station + 2cm	Comment on the UK caesarean section rate rise	Justify 'fetal CTG is unnecessary in uncomplicated low risk labour'

	Q1	Q2	Q3	Q4	Q5
Sept 1998	Debate 'perinatal mortality from Rhesus iso-immunisation should be in the past'	Advise on vulval herpes simplex infection affecting mode of delivery	Management of one twin death at 32 weeks	Manoeuvres to manage shoulder dystocia	Advise newly pregnant school canteen worker worried about acquired workplace infections affecting her baby
March 1999	Counsel parents on abdominal wall defect at 17 weeks	Treatments for idiopathic polyhydramnios at 26 weeks	Specific risks for pregnant (24 weeks) known drug-abuser	Management of a planned pregnancy of a known epileptic	Reducing ill-effects of vaginal delivery upon pelvic floor & perineum
Sept 1999	Counsel for fetus with ascites, pleural effusions & generalised oedema at 20 weeks	Minimising risk of thrombo-embolism in pregnancy	Managing slow progress during active phase of the first stage	Antenatal & intrapartum care for obese patient	Management of a first eclamptic fit after delivery

	Q1	Q2	Q3	Q4	Q5
March 2000	Decade since goal of comparable pregnancy outcome in diabetic women – achieved? & further measures needed	Management of baby with a single choroid plexus cyst found at 18 weeks	Managing pregnancy & delivery with diagnosis of autoimmune thrombocytopenia (ITP)	Care of newly pregnant woman with congenital heart disease	7 days after due date, no complications or high risk factors – advise timing of induction
Sept 2000	Critical comment on protocol for prophylaxis to reduce GBS morbidity / mortality	Management of spontaneous rupture of membranes at 30 weeks	Management of worsening generalised pruritus from 28 to 32 weeks	Management of heavy bleeding per vaginam 15 minutes after normal delivery	Critical comment on the place of version for singleton breech pregnancy

18

	Q1	Q2	Q3	Q4	Q5
March 2001	Beta thalassaemia trait marrying same ethnic background pre-conception counselling	Investigations & management for thyroid enlargement & thyrotoxicosis in middle trimester	Multiply bruised woman, haematologically normal, attends with partner. How would you deal with the situation?	Counsel elective caesarean request based on belief first child's cerebral palsy caused by intrapartum hypoxia	Establishing cause of late intrauterine death when autopsy declined
Sept 2001	Initial assessment of woman (third pregnancy, 30 weeks) midwife suspects fetus is small for dates	Critically evaluate routine antenatal HIV testing	Well-controlled pre-eclampsia at 36½ weeks in 2nd pregnancy. 1st ended in elective caesarean for breech presentation. Management when hospital guidelines indicate delivery.	Counsel on options for Downs screening (8 weeks pregnant)	Early management & diagnostic steps when 15 minutes after delivery mother suddenly becomes breathless, cyanosed & loses consciousness

19

	Q1	Q2	Q3	Q4	Q5
March 2002	Risks for known drug-abuser attending antenatal booking clinic	Minimising perinatal morbidity / mortality in multiple pregnancy	Management of echogenic bowel at 20 weeks	Discuss routine pregnancy dating	Management of a first eclamptic fit after delivery
Sept 2002	Evaluate contribution of psychiatric illness to maternal mortality & risk reduction	Management of inpatient stay due to left leg rapidly warm, swollen & painful at 16 weeks	Methods to assess fetal status in pregnancies complicated by Anti-D antibodies	Management of painful vesicular vulval eruption at 28 weeks	Management of an obese primigravida with glycosuria in early pregnancy
March 2003	Management of a tear during a normal delivery that midwife suspects has extended to anal sphincter	Advise woman, 28 weeks, 1st pregnancy, planning to fly 10 hours to a tropical country	Management of pregnant woman who has been in contact with chickenpox (varicella)	Management of antenatal care & delivery, major degree of placenta praevia at 35 weeks	Management of suspected rupture of the membranes at 17 weeks following karyotyping amniocentesis

	Q1	Q2	Q3	Q4	Q5
Sept 2003	Management of teacher at 15 weeks with outbreak of parvovirus infection in her class	Anticipation of shoulder dystocia & maternal & neonatal consequences	Pregnancy & childbirth management changes due to extreme obesity	Counsel healthy primigravida with no complications on relative merits of vaginal delivery & elective caesarean section	Implications & management of woman with a choroid plexus cyst found at 20 weeks
March 2004	Describe appropriate administration of Anti-D Immunoglobulin	Investigation & management of haemoglobin of 7.8 g/dl at 28 weeks	Diagnosis & management of generalised itching but no skin rash at 32 weeks	Management of inability to void following epidural analgesia, forceps delivery & removal of urinary catheter	Changes to care due to youth of a newly-pregnant 16-year-old
September 2004	Healthy confirmed HIV+ 23yr para1 – how modify antenatal care, delivery & postnatal care?	23yo prim possible hyperemesis at 9 weeks. How assess severity? Management when significant.	Heavy bleed 20 mins after normal delivery. Organise your team and tasks of next 30 mins:	25yo epileptic – modifications prior to and during pregnancy.	Investigations and treatment options for a 4cm fibroid.

	Q1	Q2	Q3	Q4	Q5
March 2005	Management options – primigravid woman at 38 weeks with breech presentation	Management & treatment options – suspected preterm labour at 28 weeks	Cervical smear showing severe dyskaryosis. Now at 26 weeks – management & implications for pregnancy	27yo at 36 weeks – pros & cons of delivery options; in first pregnancy had a caesarean.	24yo with MRSA nasal colonisation – principles of care, modifications to antenatal care, delivery & postnatal care
September 2005	Advise request for induction at 39 weeks for 'personal reasons'	Amniocentesis (sister had Down syndrome baby) - tests available & risks	Identifying mothers at risk of psychiatric disorder & minimising risks	Assisted delivery for maternal exhaustion – management & instrument choice	Sore left breast from expressing milk – assessment, investigation & further management.
March 2006	Mother weighs 140kg (BMI 42) - antenatal care & labour	SE Asian mother has bloods - Hepatitis B surface antigen positive (HBsAg) and e antigen negative (HBeAg). Risks & minimising them during & after pregnancy	Acute abdominal pain at 22 weeks with 3 days of vomiting – initial history, examination & investigation	Uncomplicated twin pregnancy in spontaneous labour at 37 weeks. She is 4cms dilated & twin 1 is cephalic – management.	At 33 weeks, fetus fundal height 28cms. Significance & justify subsequent antenatal care.

	Q1	Q2	Q3	Q4
September 2006	Healthy 41yo mother – fetal abnormality risks, reducing them, risks to her health & adjustments to antenatal care	Para 1 had severe pre-eclampsia, delivered at 26 weeks. Risk of recurrence, management & delivery plan.	PROM at 38 weeks: Risk status, management if low, active management methods.	Placenta undelivered after 30 mins. Info & action required of Labour ward team, further management, principles of manual removal
March 2007	Light vag bleeding at 37 weeks. Low anterior placenta – initial assessment to confirm diagnosis, investigations & complications advice before CS.	Domestic violence – alerting signs, strategies to increase detection rate & management.	Stillborn child at term – investigations & why, management before discharge.	Acute severe chest pain & shortness of breath postpartum – initial assessment, beside investigations leading to differential diagnosis & continuing management

Essay topics September 1997 – March 2007 – Paper 2

	Q6	Q7	Q8	Q9	Q10
Sept 1997	Pros & cons of sub-total abdominal hysterectomy	Cause & management of severe ovarian hyperstimulation syndrome	Justify colposcopy at 14 weeks & diathermy loop excision for severe dyskaryosis	Debate use of GnRH analogues for bilateral ovarian endometriomata	Pros & cons of HRT after hysterectomy & oophorectomy for stage IB endometrial cancer
March 1998	Identify & minimising high risk of venous thromboembolism following gynae surgery	Prognostic factors in choriocarcinoma	Non-contraceptive advantages of combined oral contraceptive pill	Treatments & natural history of vulval intra-epithelial neoplasia	Hormonal treatments for idiopathic menorrhagia

	Q6	Q7	Q8	Q9	Q10
Sept 1998	Diagnosis of pelvic pain	Objectives of surgical treatment for ovarian epithelial cancer	Treating ectopic pregnancy	Advice upon change of copper IUCD having missed the occasional period in the last year	Potential urological consequences of hysterectomy & avoiding them
March 1999	Morbidity & side-effects of chemotherapy for ovarian epithelial cancers	Promoting best possible outcomes for gynae operation abdominal incisions	Assess place of endometrial ablution for idiopathic menorrhagia	Evaluate effect of contraception on subsequent fertility	Diagnosis of abdominal pain & vaginal bleeding when period overdue
Sept 1999	Recognising & minimising laparoscopy bowel damage	Reducing risk to physical health of mother for surgical termination at 8 weeks	Management when smear suggests cervical intraepithelial glandular neoplasia (CIGN)	Management of primary dysmenorrhoea in a 16-year-old virgin	Advice on request for emergency (postcoital) contraception from a first time 17-year-old who used no contraception

	Q6	Q7	Q8	Q9	Q10
March 2000	Management of 4cm asymptomatic ovarian cyst	Debate routine genital tract Chlamydia screening	Management of complaint of urinary frequency, nocturia, urgency & urge incontinence but no other symptoms	Implications of oligomenorrhoea with polycystic ovarian disease	Pros & cons of HRT for one year post-menopausal asymptomatic 50-year-old
Sept 2000	Investigations for recurrent first trimester miscarriages	Bleeding one year after abdominal hysterectomy	Factors influencing using bilateral oophorectomy for an abdominal hysterectomy for benign disease	Management of lichen sclerosus	Investigations & immediate management of 8-year-old with breast development & menstruation
March 2001	Assessment of a 15-year-old not menstruating but otherwise apparently normal development	Evaluate oral progestogen as a single agent for menstrual cycle disorders	Management of painful intercourse three months after a vaginal delivery	Investigations & management of endometrial hyperplasia	Management of bilateral peritubal adhesions & infertility

	Q6	Q7	Q8	Q9	Q10
Sept 2001	Explain & relieve symptoms of urinary leakage 6 weeks after open Burch colposuspension for genuine stress incontinence	Treatment of symptomatic vaginal vault prolapse many years after abdominal total hysterectomy	Information to preconception clinic patient after finding 8cm uterine fibroid	Surgical management of invasive squamous cell carcinoma without metastasis	Explain & manage triplet pregnancy following IVF
March 2002	Management of a complete hydatidiform mole	Management of 52-year-old postmenopausal women with strong family osteoporosis history	Causes, investigations & therapies for anovulation	Management of slight vaginal bleeding at 9 weeks, 10mm fetus with no heart pulsations	Management of severe dysmenorrhoea symptoms, resistant to simple medical therapy

	Q6	Q7	Q8	Q9	Q10
Sept 2002	Reducing need for & risks of perioperative blood transfusion	Pros & cons of subtotal hysterectomy for dysfunctional uterine bleeding	Management of excessive facial hair	Further reducing incidence of cervical cancer in the UK	Management of postmenopausal bleeding – 15mm endometrial thickness with no other abnormalities
March 2003	Palliative care in gynae oncology	Treatment options for tubal pregnancy	Diagnosis & symptom relief of premenstrual tension	Management of complaint of urinary frequency, nocturia, urgency & urge incontinence but no other symptoms	Evaluate ultrasound, endometrial biopsy & hysteroscopy in investigating postmenopausal bleeding
Sept 2003	Management of lichen sclerosus	Safe laparascopic entry	Management of IUCD thread no longer visible	Implications of oligomenorrhoea with polycystic ovarian disease	Informed consent

	Q6	Q7	Q8	Q9	Q10
March 2004	Management of admission for severe acute pelvic inflammatory disease	Management of breakthrough bleeding while on combined oral contraceptive pill	Management options for endometrial hyperplasia	Short-term management of slight vaginal bleeding, 4mm fetus with no heart pulsations	Management of distressed rape victim who requests no police involvement
Sept 2004	Effectiveness of investigations used to evaluate recurrent first trimester miscarriage	Management of pregnancy and delivery with significant glycosuria	Ovarian cyst – factors which decide expectant management / laparoscopic surgery / laparotomy	Premature ovarian failure – diagnosis, causes, investigations & treatment	52yo on HRT for 2 years for troublesome menopause symptoms – worried about breast cancer risks – help informed choice

	Q6	Q7	Q8	Q9	Q10
March 2005	Importance & aetiology of adhesions in gynaecology & minimising them	36yo currently on COCP, sister has been treated for VTE; risk assessment & hormonal contraception options	Endometrial cancer – initial management, subsequent treatment & long-term prognosis	68yo vaginal vault prolapse many years after a hysterectomy – factors influencing management & surgical treatment options	57yo – management of lichen sclerosus
September 2005	Non-medical treatment options for incapacitating heavy periods	PCOS infertility – management & minimising of risks	Relations suffered ovarian cancer – risk, risk reduction & future implications	Stress incontinence – assessment & non-surgical management options	Failure of sterilisation with Filshie clips – factors & steps to reduce
March 2006	Principles of prophylactic antibiotics & critically assess the indications for usage in O & G	Turner syndrome – principles of management, through adolescence into adult life	Histology reports complete hydatidiform mole, 2 weeks after suction evacuation of the uterus for an incomplete miscarriage - management	Discuss & justify the surgical technique required for safe laparoscopic entry	Excessive facial and body hair & normal hormone profile. Examination, principles of management & treatment options

	Q5	Q6	Q7	Q8
September 2006	Tubal pregnancy: Indications & management approach for expectant / medical / surgical treatment	Dyspareunia, 6 months after vaginal delivery. Relevant features from delivery & puerperium, other causes & examination.	37yo - Hb of 8.7g%, heavy regular periods, 15-week size fibroid uterus – management / non-surgical / surgical	Perforation of uterus – immediate management & post-op care
March 2007	15-month history of lower abdominal pain – possible causes & features determining most likely, general principles of management	19yo sexually active for 3 months without protection, concerned about unwanted pregnancy – factors in history and examination affecting counselling and treatment options, pros & cons of emergency contraception options	Palliative care in gynae oncology – principles, pain control methods & common symptoms & their alleviation	14 days following hysterectomy urine draining from vault – possible leakage sites, how could they have been damaged, features & investigations determining site, treatment options

September 2007

Question 1:

A woman presents at 30 weeks in her first pregnancy with possible spontaneous rupture of the membranes.

A. Describe how you would establish the diagnosis: (3marks)
B. Discuss the value of further tests and monitoring of the pregnancy: (7 marks)
C. Discuss possible therapies and interventions: (10 marks)

Question 2:

A 25-year-old primigravida is 8 weeks pregnant. She has been referred early for antenatal care because she has severe (Type 3) Von Willebrand's disease.

A. What details of her Von Willebrand's disease would you need to know? (6 marks)
B. Discuss the role of prenatal diagnosis: (3 marks)
C. Discuss relevant additional management in the antenatal period because of her condition: (5 marks)
D. Discuss relevant management around the time of birth because of the condition: (6 marks)

Question 3:

A 29-year-old woman who has had Type 1 diabetes mellitus for 18 years comes to see you wanting to plan her first pregnancy.

A. What aspects of her medical condition could impact upon her pregnancy? (7 marks)
B. Detail the general advice you would give her: (6 marks)
C. What outcomes are you aiming to improve by preconceptual care? (7 marks)

Question 4:

You are called to the labour ward for a woman who has just sustained an anal sphincter injury following a normal delivery.

A. Discuss the principles of repair of anal sphincter injuries: (9 marks)
B. Discuss immediate and long term postoperative care: (6 marks)
C. What advice would you give with regard to future pregnancies? (5 marks)

Question 5:

A 15-year-old girl presents to the gynaecology clinic with a complaint of painful periods. Her GP has tried a non-steroidal anti-inflammatory drug and the contraceptive pill without success.

A. What factors in the social history are particularly relevant to her management? (6 marks)
B. Discuss what investigations should be considered: (6 marks)
C. Assuming the diagnosis is of primary dysmenorrhoea, what treatment options should be considered? (8 marks)

Question 6:

A 26-year-old woman is admitted a day after oocyte retrieval for IVF with a history of abdominal pain and distension, and shortness of breath.

A. Discuss the differential diagnosis: (5 marks)
B. Justify what investigations you would perform: (6 marks)
C. Outline your management plan: (9 marks)

Question 7:

The incidence of cervical cancer in the UK has fallen dramatically since the introduction of the cervical screening programme.

A. What are the organisational elements that have made the screening programme successful? (7 marks)
B. What are the limitations of the national screening programme? (6 marks)
C. Explain how recent developments in prophylaxis and diagnostics may help to reduce the incidence further: (7 marks)

Question 8:

Non-absorbable materials are now commonly used during pelvic floor surgery to support the tissues.

A. Which procedures use these materials and why have these procedures gained acceptance? (8 marks)
B. What are the common and serious complications when using these materials and how do they present? (6 marks)
C. What can be done to reduce the risk of these complications? (6 marks)

Question 1:

A woman with monochorionic twins presents at 22 weeks with a rapid increase in abdominal distension. You suspect twin-to-twin transfusion syndrome.

A. What features assist in making the diagnosis and assessing the severity of the problem? (9 marks)

B. If twin-to-twin transfusion syndrome is confirmed, critically appraise the management options at this gestation: (11 marks)

Question 2:

There has been an increase in the number of cases of amniotic fluid embolism reported in the last triennium. The condition can present in a number of ways.

A. What are the clinical criteria required for a diagnosis of amniotic fluid embolism? (5 marks)

B. Discuss how to optimise the initial management of this condition: (5 marks)

C. One of the presenting features of an amniotic fluid embolism is an acute seizure. Discuss the differential diagnosis and how you identify the cause: (10 marks)

Question 3:

A 30-year-old woman has a history of one prior caesarean section and wishes to deliver vaginally in this pregnancy.

A. How would you counsel the woman antenatally about the risks of vaginal birth after Caesarean section (VBAC)? (8 marks)

B. Discuss the factors in her past obstetric history that may influence the decision to undergo VBAC? (5 marks)

C. What measures will you undertake to achieve an optimum clinical outcome? (7 marks)

Question 4:

A nulliparous woman with a singleton pregnancy presents at 33 weeks' gestation with intense 'itching' of her hands and feet.

A. Discuss the differential diagnosis: (4 marks)
B. Discuss the features on physical examination (1 mark) and the investigations (7 marks) that may assist in making the diagnosis:
C. If the diagnosis is confirmed as obstetric cholestasis, justify your management options: (8 marks)

Question 5:

A 34-year-old man is referred to your clinic with a semen analysis reported as showing azospermia.

A. Describe the salient features in the male history and examination which may point to a diagnosis: (8 marks)
B. State the investigations you would perform, and discuss how each result would help you determine the cause of the azospermia: (7 marks)
C. Briefly outline the possible treatment options: (5 marks)

Question 6:

A 62-year-old women presents in the outpatient clinic with persistent vulval irritation. Examination reveals areas of vulval skin atrophy and superficial ulceration together with white plaques of skin thickening.

A. What other factors would you wish to highlight in her history? (9 marks)
B. What would be the most useful investigations? (4 marks)
C. If neoplasia is subsequently excluded, outline her immediate (4 marks) and long-term management: (3 marks)

Question 7:

A 53-year-old woman is referred with symptoms of frequently 'being wet' in association with urinary urgency, frequency, and nocturia.

A. Discuss the relevance of any investigations which should be performed before commencing treatment: (7 marks)
B. Discuss the non-pharmacological treatment options for an overactive bladder: (13 marks)

Question 8:

A 28-year-old nulliparous woman presents with threatened miscarriage. A scan confirms an intrauterine intact gestational sac, a crown rump length equivalent to 7 weeks' gestation and no fetal heartbeat.

A. Critically evaluate the clinical management options with particular reference to complications including failure rates: (13 marks)
B. What may influence her options? (4 marks)
C. What specific advice would you give her with regards to future pregnancy? (3 marks)

September 2008

Question 1:

A 30-year-old woman who is known to be HIV positive books for antenatal care in her first pregnancy.

A. What specific measures should be taken during her antenatal care? (10 marks)
B. How should her delivery be managed? (8 marks)
C. What other measures would minimise mother to child transmission of HIV? (2 marks)

Question 2:

A. In the first stage of spontaneous labour in a low risk woman, when do you diagnose a 'delay in labour' and what additional findings should be taken into account? (5 marks)
B. Discuss the factors affecting management when there is delay in the first stage of labour: (7 marks)
C. Discuss the management of delay in the first stage of labour: (8 marks)

Question 3:

A 20-year-old pregnant patient with hypertrophic cardiomyopathy presents for antenatal care. Discuss the investigation and management of this patient.

A. In the prenatal period: (9 marks)
B. During labour and delivery: (7 marks)
C. Postnatally: (4 marks)

Question 4:

A 25-year-old woman in her first pregnancy books for antenatal care at 12 weeks' amenorrhoea with a body mass index (BMI) over 40 kg/m2.

A. Given her obesity, justify what specific measures should be taken during her antenatal care: (8 marks)
B. How would you manage her labour (9 marks) and early postnatal period (3 marks)?

Question 5:

A 30-year-old woman is seen in the Early Pregnancy Unit. She is pregnant for the first time and a tubal pregnancy is diagnosed. She is haemodynamically stable. Outline the indications for and the management approach for the following treatment options:

A. Expectant (6 marks)
B. Medical (8 marks)
C. Surgical (6 marks)

Question 6:

A 28-year-old nulliparous woman presents with postcoital bleeding. Colposcopic examination suggests she has cervical carcinoma.

A. Describe your initial assessment to establish the diagnosis, justifying the procedures performed: (6 marks)
B. Outline how a management plan would be prepared, and discuss what factors influence the treatment options: (9 marks)
C. She has recently married and is keen to preserve fertility. Briefly discuss what potential options are available: (5 marks)

Question 7:

A 29-year-old nulliparous woman presents with menstrual related pain. Transvaginal ultrasound demonstrates bilateral ovarian cysts of approximately 6 cm with a typical appearance of endometriomas.

A. Discuss what additional information is helpful in assessing the most appropriate treatment: (9 marks)
B. How would you counsel the woman about her management options? (11 marks)

Question 8:

A 65-year-old woman presents with a vaginal bulge, 20 years after undergoing a hysterectomy. On pelvic examination she has a stage IV vault prolapse.

A. Describe what specific symptoms are relevant in assessing this patient's prolapse: (5 marks)
B. Critically evaluate the abdominal (8 marks) and vaginal (7 marks) surgical options used to treat grade IV prolapse:

EXTENDED MATCHING QUESTIONS

Extended matching questions (EMQs) are designed to probe a candidate's understanding of a subject and hence enhance validity of the test. They contain at least four options per list of options. Often, the number of options is much more than four, up to a maximum of twenty. There are thus 20 spaces lettered A to T to fill in on the answer sheet. In this way, it becomes more difficult to guess the correct answer. In a MCQ there is an even chance that someone with almost no knowledge would choose the correct answer!

As far as reasonably possible the lists of options are made homogeneous. Most options will be broadly equivalent or at least in similar areas. The option lists will nearly always be in alphabetical or numerical order for ease of reference; if not, they will be in the most appropriate order for quick reference.

Each EMQ consists of the following three components;

1. A list of options
2. A lead in statement which explains the scenario and acts as the bridge between the list of options and the items
3. The items themselves.

The lead-in statement is designed to link the items with the options and clarify the issues and task required for you as much as possible. Please do read it carefully - it may change the answer – for example choosing an option that is a 'management' for the question scenario may be totally different from the option you should choose as an 'initial management'.

A number of the items will have quite substantial clinical scenarios to interpret. The essential domains of management, diagnosis and investigation will be the most frequently tested and reflecting the enlarging scope of the specialty candidates will also be tested on statistics, interpretation of data, audit, genetics and pharmacology. As with the MCQs, there is no negative marking; no marks are deducted for incorrect answers.

Each EMQ paper in the Part 2 MRCOG would contain exactly 40 items based around (usually) 18 lists of options. Some of the lists of options would only lead to one item; most will have two or three items.

The website mrcogadvantage.com contains five EMQ papers at the present time. Therefore, there are 200 items which would provide well over six hours of test time for practise. I would recommend that you ensure you have enough uninterrupted time for taking each paper. The EMQ papers can be taken one at a time and I would advise that you take the papers one at a time spread across several evenings or weekends.

So what are the main differences between EMQs and the more familiar types of formats for assessment?
With the wider number of options available, it is obvious that the educated guess becomes a far less valuable technique than in the 50:50 world of the true or false MCQ. That doesn't mean that an educated guess is not sometimes appropriate for EMQs. Essentially, for the EMQ paper, your guessing needs to be judicious. As with the true / false MCQ paper, there is no negative marking. However, even 'good guessing' may well lead to an unsustainably high number of mistakes in the EMQ paper. While EMQs do not reach the levels of synthesis of clinical knowledge that can be tested in the SAQs, they do test more complex understanding than MCQs. Simple recall of knowledge suffices for correctly answering many true / false MCQs. This will continue to apply to some EMQs but most will require some working through. Solid, applied clinical knowledge will be required to answer the majority of EMQs. A number will have quite substantial clinical scenarios to interpret. In recognition of their increased length and complexity, in particular with regard to the extra time required to read them, EMQs have been assigned a longer time for completion than MCQs. Indeed, in a rare response to popular candidate demand, the College has even increased this time by 15 minutes recently. This is very important to bear in mind when preparing.

You should find this technique useful in tackling EMQs:

1. Read the 'lead in' statement first.
2. Ask yourself the question – 'Do I really understand what the 'lead in' statement says?
3. Consider each item one by one.
4. Develop the answer to the item in your mind.
5. Finally, select the correct answer from the list of options and enter your answer into the mark sheet.

Again – perhaps oddly at first sight – I do not advise that you read through the list of options first. There is a small but live possibility of being wrongly cued by distractors among the options by doing this. The 'lead in' statement will generally be very clear as to the task required and should leave no room for ambiguity. Reading it carefully and understanding it will be the key to performing the task required in the right manner and thus answering the question correctly. Then, for candidates with an appropriate standard of knowledge and experience, it should be a simple matter to answer the items.

E
M
Q

MULTIPLE CHOICE QUESTIONS

The 90 minutes MCQ paper has 225 questions, of which approximately half are obstetrics and half gynaecology. The format is usually a statement, topic or clinical scenario followed by a varying number of items (typically between one and five), all of which have to be rated as true or false.

With the binary choice of just true or false, the MCQs are by a substantial margin a simpler format than the other two formats to get to grips with. Having said that, they should not be ignored – after all they hold 25% of the written marks and the format should be practised. Moreover the MCQ papers will draw on the full range of your knowledge of obstetrics and gynaecology – often quite far and wide. The MCQs will range across more areas compared to the EMQs and SAQs which tend to concentrate on the main, core problems, while the MCQs can, albeit briefly and not generally too searchingly, touch on the more obscure and rare areas of the Part 2 curriculum.

What are my main hints and tips for them?

    a.   Read the subject matter carefully
    b.   Allow plenty of time for revision
    c.   Practise specimen papers
    d.   Read the MCQ very carefully before you apply pencil to paper.

These may seem rather familiar, but my next point may strike some of you as rather counter-intuitive, and somewhat contradictory to my last point. This is to back your hunches. The first answer you think of is likely to be correct. There is even a growing pool of research confirming this - studies demonstrate that even in negatively marked MCQ papers (which the Part 2 MCQ is not) all candidates should benefit substantially from backing their educated guesses and only a small percentage lose marks by backing their wild guesses. For lots of fun and mostly non-medical examples, see the non-fiction bestseller, Malcolm Gladwell's Blink: The Power of Thinking Without Thinking. Similarly, the questions range from easy to hard, so don't be anxious if the answer appears obvious - you are probably correct.

M
C
Q

There is no negative marking, so you are not penalised for guessing and it is entirely in your interest to fill up absolutely every lozenge on the answer sheet – even if some are guessed they have a 50:50 chance of being correct and gaining a mark.

None of the questions are meant to be trick questions. It is unlikely that a question will be based around only one set of data (e.g., a single paper), therefore base your answers on recent reviews, text books, the Cochrane Database, RCOG 'Green-top' guidelines etc.

Answer directly onto the marking sheet; this saves time and avoids transcription errors.
Rub out mistakes fully - the electronic scanner used for marking will not allocate a mark if it appears that two boxes are completed. Work systematically through the questions and answer those you know; then attempt the questions you found difficult. Don't go back over the questions already answered, unless there is a specific piece of information you have remembered.

There are ten past Part 2 MCQ papers (1997-2001) that have been published in a compendium by the RCOG Press under the ISBN 978-1-904752-03-5. Many remain in the question bank and will reappear from time to time. The answers are not included – both to discourage rote-learning and to encourage self-directed learning. It hardly needs stating that working through these will pay big dividends. Indeed generally only between a quarter to a third of the questions will be totally new and fresh for each sitting, although as 2002-8 papers have not been published, the vast majority of questions are not in the public domain. **http://www.rcog.org.uk/index.asp?PageID=73&BookCategoryI D=6&BookTypeID=63&BookDetailsID=1338.**

PASSING THE PART 2 ORAL ASSESSMENT

What is it?

You will notice that this examination seems to be referred to interchangeably as the oral assessment and as an OSCE. Both names are worth bearing in mined. It is an oral assessment, so all the marks you will be awarded will be gained from your spoken answers (there are some rare exceptions to this - see below).

It is also an OSCE - that is objective structured clinical examination. Objective means that marks are awarded for the specific and relevant knowledge that you display in the oral stations and for your skill and judgement at communicating it. Examiners cannot engage in off-topic chit-chat ('Did you come far?', 'Who have you trained under?' etc) as this would sway their marking subjectively. If stations end early, there is therefore an awkward but necessary silence.

Structured means that, while not fully scripted, examiners and role players will be bound by a tightly structured marking sheet. This will be noticeable at times. You may start a line of questioning, management advice, or such-like that you think will be useful, but in response the examiner or role player is pretty much blank, overly non-committal, or even gives you a gentle steer to a different topic. Take the hint! There will not be marks in the area you are pursuing.

Clinical means that it focuses on clinical cases. Remember to convey a significant amount of clinical material on most of the stations.

Examination we will take as read. It is a challenging and very stressful example of a test. However, it is not an impossible exam by any means and the pass rate is usually in the range of 70 -80%.

The rare exceptions to the "all marks awarded are gained from your spoken answers" rule are as follows;

There are some very rare stations where you have to teach a skill such as knot-tying, instrumental or ventouse delivery to an actress or actor playing the role of a junior doctor. Here there will be a few 'non-spoken marks' to be gained, although the vast majority will continue to

O
S
C
E

47

be gained by your spoken teaching to the role-player. You will be given a few marks however for your own skill and dexterity at the task when you are demonstrating it.

The Circuit

You will go round and be marked on ten stations. These can be divided into:
*   role playing stations where an actress plays the part of a patient (or much more rarely an actor plays the part of a patient's partner)
*   interactive stations with the examiner.

Nearly always, the nature of the station will be stated in the first or second line of the candidate's instructions on the outside of the station.

At each you have 14 minutes of active examining time, preceded by one minute to read the question outside the station. The boundaries are marked by beeping buzzers. You nearly always go round the circuits clockwise in order - 1 to 2, 2 to 3 and so on until 12 where you go on to 1. You can however start at any one of these and the number of the first station would be stated on your entry slip. Make sure you start at the right station.

Two of these stations will be preparatory (normally stations 2 and 9) where you will have 14 minutes to look at and organise some larger cases - often sets of full case notes, a heavier number (8 to 10) of shorter cases, a labour ward board or operations prioritisation task. These preparatory stations are also useful for resting, re-focusing and (hopefully unnecessary) taking a brief toilet break.

Recently, the circuits have consisted of five interactive stations and five with a role player. A balance of 6 of one and 4 of the other in either direction is also possible, but anything more unbalanced than this is very unlikely. Each station is marked out of 20. It is not essential to pass all the stations or one in particular. An overall pass mark is needed in the oral assessment to obtain the MRCOG. The pass mark usually ranges between 114 and 120 - i.e. between 57% and 60%. A candidate should aim for a mark of 120 (60%) to be confident of passing the examination. Your score in the written paper is not carried through to the oral. The oral stands alone - you have a fresh slate. Only the Gold Medal is awarded on a combined score.

Role-playing stations

At a role-play station, you will meet with, interact with and generally counsel a professional actress playing the part of a patient. Rarely, a male role player may be used to play a patient's partner. Stations with a patient and a partner as a couple and a male infertility station have not yet arisen in the modern OSCE (i.e. since 1997) but they are not totally outside the realms of possibility.

Each station will have a set of instructions setting out the clinical scenario. Often there will be a series of bullet points at the end of these instructions listing a few tasks. If there are, pay particular attention to them and arrange your answers around them - generally in order - as you will be marked on your ability to address them. The examiner will be a 'fly on the wall'; they will take no part in the station apart from awarding your marks. Generally, unlike the viva stations, no further information other than that provided orally by the role player will be available. If examination findings are given in the instructions, then that is exactly what the question is testing. Take those findings as being true; if these instructions do not outline a physical examination, then unless it is clearly irrelevant it would be worth asking the role player about it. They will have been given appropriate instructions, to deal with the question depending on its relevance – they may give a brief description of a previous physical examination or 'blank' the question. If the latter, you can safely assume that the examination findings are normal, as with test results. It is important to appreciate that the appearance of the role player may not correspond exactly to the patient they are simulating. (Naturally, they are generally actresses in the early stages of their careers.) As a result it is very important to read the question instructions, especially with regard to age, body mass index and the like, carefully as they may well be quite or considerably different to that of the 'patient' in front of you. However, the role-player will have been given a structured 'brief' about the patient they are representing. They may also have a series of questions that will need to be addressed, or a series of prompts to keep the candidate on the right track.

O
S
C
E

The main types of questions that will involve the use of a role player include:
* breaking bad news: bad news can be simply defined as information that the patient is not expecting and which upsets her. For overseas candidates, the UK style of breaking bad news may well be quite different to your local practice; there are many courses available in the UK on breaking bad news and if you feel you are lacking in this area, I would strongly recommend that you attend a relevant course. Much good practice such as involving partners, family or friends is, of course, impossible to replicate in the OSCE stations.
There will usually be a station dealing with breaking bad news in most oral exams. In most of these scenarios, it is important to understand that clinical situations are chosen in which there would be no doubt about the diagnosis. Don't waste time on this aspect. In obstetrics, a typical scenario to expect may involve a fetal abnormality picked up on an ultrasound scan, which may or may not be incompatible with extrauterine life or the need to deliver early. In gynaecology, the bad news may be a diagnosis of cancer, pre cancer or the inability to become pregnant. Whichever scenario is used, one of your main tasks will be to effectively communicate the options that may be open to the patient / role player. In these stations it is hard to strike the right balance between being overly positive or negative - be realistic and as straightforward about the diagnosis as possible.

Two useful pieces of advice for this type of station are:
1. Use diagrams to explain diagnoses and options
2. Allow the role player time to ask questions. In other words, accept short silences, however uncomfortable they may feel before moving on. Use of supportive, professional questions like 'Do you understand?', 'Are you OK to move on and talk about some other aspects?' will be rewarding.

* counselling a patient to discuss a diagnosis and, or treatment or management options: this type of station may involve a preparatory station with a set of notes for the patient. It may involve debriefing the role player after an untoward incident while in hospital, discussing clinical results and subsequent management options open to the patient. It cannot be emphasised enough that the candidate needs to read the question carefully and to fully address the appropriate bullet points. A major pitfall with this type of question is that the candidate

reverts to the comfort zone of history taking and does not address the issues in the question.

* communicating or interpreting information: a common type of this scenario will involve the patient bringing in information from the internet **(often altered purposely to be misguided and inaccurate)** to discuss her further management options. A preparatory station is usual to allow the candidate to read and assess the information. The information will be relevant to the tasks required in the question.

* History taking: this is a core skill and I would expect it to be included as the first part of some multi part OSCE stations in every oral examination. It is likely to occur twice in any one examination. A station which has history taking as its main focus is also highly likely. In addition, a number of other stations may also have history taking as a quick preliminary task scoring 2 to 4 marks. It is surprising that, although one would expect this type of station and task to enable high scores, with most candidates picking up the majority of the marks available, the opposite is true. Essential elements of the history taking are often omitted by candidates, which very often leads to the subsequent parts of the question being poorly answered. In the UK, midwives undertake most obstetric booking histories and this may reflect the poor performance of many candidates. In preparation, you are advised to appraise the limitations of your own history taking and practice it extensively and self-critically.

* Practical skills or teaching: teaching is part of the curriculum and is best assessed in an OSCE setting. A good exercise for candidates to use in their preparation for this type of question is to teach medical students or doctors junior to themselves. If a skill is being demonstrated, candidates need to demonstrate that skill, take the role player through it and then to ask them to undertake it alone.

O
S
C
E

Interactive vivas with the examiner

These are types of question which do not use a role-play and so only involve the examiner and the candidate. The main types are as follows:
* Prioritisation exercise: usually there will be a preparatory station to enable the candidate to go through the information before meeting the examiner. In obstetrics, this may be a labour ward board to assess. In gynaecology, it may be a waiting list. It is important that, irrespective of the candidate's approach to the question, no case is omitted. The examiners are advised not to prompt and marks will therefore not be awarded to cases that the candidate has not discussed. The candidate needs to understand the meanings of NHS target times. Target waits refer to suspected cancers and a diagnosis needs to be made within 31 days of referral and treatment commenced within 62 days. As a generalisation, "urgent wait" means within 4 weeks and "routine" wait is 18 weeks from being placed on the waiting list. This may change again with continuing NHS reforms. Check that you are up-to-date with this knowledge.
* Dealing with emergencies: these emergencies will usually be common problems encountered in clinical practice, including bleeding, fitting or collapse in obstetrics and gynaecology. It is useful for the candidate to have attended at least one of the following: an Advanced Life Support in Obstetrics (ALSO) course, a Management of Obstetric Emergencies and Trauma (MOET) or a local 'drills & skills' session in preparation for this type of station. However there is no substitute for adequate clinical experience.
* Interpreting results: the candidate may be required to consider what further information is necessary, giving a diagnosis or discussing further management options. The results for the most part will be straightforward with no hidden catches. A useful exercise is to go through results that may be sent to your consultant after a patient's clinic visit, or watch OSCEs for the MRCOG Made Easy Volumes 1 & 2.
* Operative surgery: over the past few years, this kind of interactive viva has become an integral part of the OSCE. The areas that the candidate may expect to be covered include the use of instruments and sutures, common gynaecological operations, as well as the uncommon but serious complications that may be encountered during surgery, such as bladder or bowel injury. Preoperative preparation in

the form of a simulated ward round discussion may also be included. On the obstetric side, it may be some form of operative delivery or repair of a complication discovered at the time of delivery.

* Protocol design/audit/risk management: clinical governance is an essential part of current medical practice. These issues may be addressed by case reviews of problems encountered during a patient's care and a review of how changes could be implemented to prevent similar problems in the future. Clinical governance will usually be covered in some manner and debriefing a role player after an untoward incident is an appropriate test. Concerning audit, the process (the audit cycle) is the same irrespective of the topic. It has become mandatory in most units for all the juniors to undertake some form of audit every 6 months. For those candidates who have not previously been exposed to audit, it would be advisable to learn the stages of the audit cycle and their application.

* Structured viva: many topics in either Obstetrics or Gynaecology, can be tested in this way. Over the past few years, the OSCE committee has tended to develop a number of these as three or four-part questions. They usually deal with a specific case at different stages of its management. One section leads on to the next but you cannot go back to change their answers. In this kind of viva, equal marks are usually awarded to each part. Actual cases are often used to maintain a realistic feel to the question.

The pass rate for those sitting the oral assessment and being awarded the MRCOG is usually in the range of 70 to 80%, and quite often near the top end. This reflects the fact that most candidates who have passed the written paper will have the knowledge, experience and ability to pass the oral assessment. Remember that, if you have found a question difficult, it is likely that other candidates will also have done so.

O
S
C
E

Pitfalls

There are a number of pitfalls which must be avoided. Lack of knowledge is not usually a major pitfall. The main ones include:

* Failure to read the instructions. This is the major reason that candidates come unstuck; by answering the question they would like to be asked rather than the actual question. The Part 2 Oral Assessment Sub-committee takes great pains to avoid ambiguity and the bullet points that are present in the instructions to Examiners are the points that will be awarded marks. Usually the marks are distributed equally throughout the sections, unless it is stated otherwise.

* Lack of clinical experience. This is obviously a major reason for failing the examination. The knowledge may be present but its application may be limited. The oral assessment is a clinical OSCE and can only be passed by candidates with the appropriate level of clinical skills.

* Poor command of English. Although a candidate's written English may be adequate, they may find difficulty with the spoken word and this may be reflected in slowness in answering questions, misunderstanding of role player's questions and difficulties in the role player's and the examiner's understanding of that candidate's speech. Watching Volumes 1 & 2 of OSCEs for the MRCOG Made Easy, will give you a form of words to use, how to say them and which non verbal cues you should demonstrate at the same time.

* Poor knowledge of UK practice. The MRCOG is a British licensing examination, which reflects UK practice. For candidates from outside the UK, practice may be different and so it is important to have a good picture of the UK system and its ramifications.

* Poor time management. Where possible, examiners will ensure that you use the time optimally and most questions are completed within the 14 minutes allotted. If there are three bullet points in a question, then equal time should be devoted to each section, unless otherwise stated.

O
S
C
E

Preparation

One of the challenging aspects of the Part 2 MRCOG examination is the time lag between the written papers and the oral assessment. It is important that you do not lose momentum, and during this time you could ensure that there are no gaps in your knowledge base. Practice in history-taking is important as these marks should be relatively easy to obtain. You can be assured that there will be a significant amount of relevant history-taking in the oral. Attendance at multidisciplinary team meetings, both obstetric and gynaecological, may prove beneficial in dealing with current practice in a discursive multi-professional manner. Attendance at clinics watching a consultant breaking bad news may also be useful if you have limited experience in that area.

O
S
C
E

Key points

* Anyone who gains a "pass" mark in the written paper and proceeds to the oral assessment has a good chance of gaining the Part 2 MRCOG examination - you've proved you have the knowledge required by passing the written test.

* Breadth of knowledge and experience are essential.

* The golden rule is to read the question thoroughly.

* Start the question as soon as you can - while continuing to meet the golden rule of reading the question thoroughly.

O
S
C
E

WORKED EXAMPLES

MCQs

Remember the four key pieces of advice I have given:

1. *Read the subject matter carefully*
2. *Allow plenty of time for revision*
3. *Practise specimen papers*
4. *Read the MCQ very carefully before you apply pencil to paper.*

Consider the first two worked examples;

---

34. The following are reassuring in an insulin dependent diabetic woman who is considering pregnancy;

A	Pre meal capillary whole blood glucose = 7.8 mmol/l	**False**
B	Pre meal capillary whole blood glucose = 4.0 mmol/l	**True**
C	Pre meal capillary whole blood glucose = 2.0 mmol/l	**False**
D	HbA1C 6%	**True**
E	HbA1C 12 %	**False**

---

35. The following are non reassuring in an insulin dependent diabetic woman who is considering pregnancy;

A	Pre meal capillary whole blood glucose = 7.8 mmol/l	**True**
B	Pre meal capillary whole blood glucose = 4.0 mmol/l	**False**
C	Pre meal capillary whole blood glucose = 2.0 mmol/l	**True**
D	HbA1C 6%	**False**
E	HbA1C 12 %	**True**

M
C
Q

The items are identical but the answers are opposite. Why is this? The use of the prefix "non" in front of "reassuring" alters the entire meaning of the question. The subject matter is straightforward. The prepregnancy care of diabetic women is important and decisive for a good outcome in pregnancy. A candidate who is familiar with this issue and who reads the MCQ carefully would have little trouble in identifying the correct answers.

Worked example 3 is an example of a knowledge based question on amniotic fluid embolism.

44. Amniotic fluid embolism;

A	Is a toxic confusional state	**True**
B	Must be considered in all cases when a woman collapses 6 hours after delivery	**False**
C	Is associated with bronchodilatation	**False**
D	Occurs most often during labour	**True**
E	Rarely occurs if the maternal age is advanced	**False**

Most candidates know that it is a toxic confusional state with acute cardio respiratory collapse, broncho-constriction and disseminated intravascular coagulation. A few have trouble with item B. The condition may occur at any time during pregnancy and within 30 minutes of the end of a pregnancy. If a woman collapses 6 hours after delivery then other causes must be considered.

Worked example 4 is an example of a MCQ which would be easy for candidates with appropriate clinical experience.

25. Cysts of Bartholin's gland;

A	Are usually bilateral	**False**
B	May become infected with Neisseria gonorrhoea	**True**
C	Lie above the pelvic diaphragm	**False**
D	May contain a small focus of air	**True**
E	Are usually more than 5 cm in diameter	**False**

A cyst of the Bartholin's gland is usually unilateral, may become infected with a sexually transmitted organism such as Neisseria gonorrhoea and contain a small focus of air. Bartholin's glands lie below the pelvic diaphragm. A cyst, as opposed to an abscess, of the Bartholin's gland is usually 1 or 2 cm in diameter.

What about rare conditions? You are more likely to encounter these in the MCQ section. It is easier to ask a few MCQs on rare conditions than devote a whole SAQ for example to one rare condition. Consider worked example 5

29. In a person with testicular feminisation;

A	Testes are absent	**False**
B	The phenotype is male	**False**
C	The karyotype is 46 XY	**True**
D	The cervix is absent	**True**
E	The uterus is absent	**True**

The candidate must understand the underlying pathophysiology. Testicular feminisation syndrome is best remembered as androgen insensitivity syndrome. The genotype is male, testes are present and androgens are produced. However, the androgens are unable to alter the development of a female phenotype as the tissues are insensitive. Peripheral conversion of androgens to oestrogens still occurs. Therefore, the affected individual has a karyotype 46XY, absent uterus and cervix, a female appearance with well developed breasts and may present as a female with primary amenorrhoea.

Worked example 6 is another MCQ about a rare condition. Again, knowledge of key facts about a rare disease will help in tackling the MCQ. Mixed Mullerian tumour occurs in elderly women and often presents as an enlarging uterine mass. It is an aggressive tumour and metastasises early. Histologically, the lesion contains tissues resembling carcinoma and sarcoma.

M
C
Q

38. Malignant mixed Mullerian tumour;

A	Contains tissues which differentiate both as carcinoma and endodermal sinus tumour	**False**
B	Occurs more commonly in prepubertal girls	**False**
C	Is usually a large aggressively invasive uterine mass	**True**
D	Is commonly associated with distant metastases at the time of diagnosis	**True**
E	Is associated with a 5 year survival rate of 5%	**False**

The good news; it is unlikely that there will be more than one MCQ for each rare condition. The MRCOG examination has to cover a lot of area.

Key Points

1. Read as much as you can in order to cover as wide an area as possible.

2. Gain as much relevant clinical experience as you can.

3. Know as much as possible about common conditions.

4. Understand as much as possible about life threatening conditions.

5. Learn three or four 'core' or basic facts about uncommon conditions.

6. Practise, practise, practise

EMQs

EMQs are demanding and can be tricky – but you should not be too daunted by them, if you get a good amount of practice at the format you should find them increasingly easier to tackle. Remember the step-wise technique that I advise:

1. *Read the 'lead in' statement first.*
2. *Ask yourself the question –*
   'Do I really understand what the 'lead in' statement says?
3. *Consider each item one by one.*
4. *Develop the answer to the item in your mind.*
5. *Finally, select the correct answer from the list of options and enter your answer on to the mark sheet.*

I hope that you find the following worked examples helpful.

Consider worked example 1.

OPTIONS
A	1
B	5
C	100
D	200
E	295
F	495
G	500
H	1000
I	5000
J	9000
K	19000
L	90000
M	99000
N	100000

A new screening system for open neural tube defects in the fetus complicating pregnancy has been developed. It is claimed that the system has a sensitivity of 99 % and a specificity of 99.5 %. You are asked for your advice on how the system will perform in practice in a region in the United Kingdom with 100,000 births per annum assuming that every pregnant woman takes up the offer of screening. It is reliably estimated that there would be 500 women who would have a pregnancy affected by this particular population. If the claims about the sensitivity and specificity are correct and the test is applied to 100,000 women choose the closest matching option for each of the items listed below. Each option may be used once, more than once or not at all.

ITEM 1
Number of pregnancies affected by open neural tube defect which would be "screen positive".

ANSWER F

ITEM 2
Number of pregnancies affected by open neural tube defect which would be "screen negative".

ANSWER B

ITEM 3
Number of pregnancies unaffected by open neural tube defect which would be "screen positive".

ANSWER G

ITEM 4
Number of pregnancies unaffected by open neural tube defect which would be "screen negative".

ANSWER M

Its very appearance may be repulsive to many candidates. But, the EMQ is based on a simple formula which candidates for Part 2 MRCOG would be well advised to remember. Furthermore, principles such as sensitivity are fundamental for a sound understanding of screening tests.

The list of options is a series of numbers. Let us ignore the list of options for a moment and read the lead in statement. The scenario is quite straightforward; you are asked to give your advice on the performance of a screening test which has a sensitivity of 99% and a specificity of 99.5% when applied to a population of pregnant women numbering approximately 100,000. The lead in statement helpfully states that there would be 500 affected women in this particular population. Several factors relevant to passing the Part 2 MRCOG come to the fore;

1. The actual nature of the condition does not matter in this particular scenario. Learn the recipe and apply for different questions.

2. The numbers which are used are actually there to help the candidate find the correct answer. The "purist" will correctly claim that 100,000 births are not equal to the number of pregnant woman and that the incidence of open neural tube defects is too high. Those considerations do not matter as far as answering the question is concerned. The Examiners wish to know whether a candidate is capable of applying principles.

3. The candidate is asked to select the "closest matching option" for the items in the EMQ.

Item 1 is another way of asking the "detection rate" for the test. What is the "detection rate"? It is the sensitivity of a screening test. In other words, if 500 women are affected, a test with a sensitivity of 99% would detect 495 women. These women would react as "screen positive" when tested. Therefore, the correct response to item 1 is F. Note that the EMQ does not ask how many women actually go on to undergo a diagnostic test. Item 1 simply asks how many affected women would be screen positive.

What about the other 5 women who are affected (500 minus 495) and who react as "screen negative" when tested? They represent the answer to item 2 which is B.

Item 3 asks the candidate to identify the number of women whose screening test results would be false positive. How can the candidate

E
M
Q

calculate this? The test has a specificity of 99.5% and therefore, 0.5% would be false positive. The number of pregnant women being screened is 100,000 and 0.5% of that number is 500. The answer is G.

How many pregnant women will have test results which are "true negatives"? We have seen from the lead in statement itself that 500 pregnant women are affected. Another 500 pregnant women will have false positive results. Therefore, 99.000 pregnant women are unaffected and they react as "screen negative". The answer is M. This is also shown by the calculation for specificity which is true negatives divided by the total number without the condition (true negatives and false positives). In this EMQ, that is 99,000/99,500 which is 99.5%.

Many candidates would actually find it easier to construct a 4 x 4 table using the figures which are provided.

	Disease present	Disease absent
Screening test +	495	500
Screening test -	5	99,000

The number of affected pregnant women (disease present) is 500 and the sensitivity is 99%. This implies that 5 will be undetected. Another 500 will be false positive leaving 99,000 true negatives. The approach is the same for all such questions which involve the application of simple principles of screening.

Worked example 2 shows how an EMQ may appear formidable but it is easier than one might think at first.

Options

A   Amniocentesis
B   Chorionic villus sampling
C   Counsel termination of pregnancy
D   Determine carrier status of partner
E   Obtain family records for linkage studies
F   Reassure that there is no risk

Select the most appropriate next step in management for the woman in the clinical scenario below.

ITEM 1

A 28 year old woman of North European ethnicity is 11 weeks into her first pregnancy and she is extremely concerned that her baby is affected by cystic fibrosis. The woman has an affected niece who is very ill and she has been identified as a gene carrier for cystic fibrosis

ANSWER   D

The list of options contains different options for management. Linkage studies? Invasive testing? If so, what is the most appropriate method? In the scenario, the candidate is presented with a pregnant woman of North European origin with a family history of cystic fibrosis. She is worried. The next step in management is to determine the carrier status of her partner. The answer is D. If her partner does not have the gene for cystic fibrosis, then the woman can be reassured that the chances of her having an affected child are low. If her partner is also a carrier, then prenatal diagnosis can be discussed. Would determination of carrier status exclude all the known mutations for cystic fibrosis? No, it will not. However, the answer is still D.

Now for a domain that seems to terrify some candidates; research methodology. The Part 2 MRCOG examination demands a simple understanding of research methods and the ability to interpret data. Worked example 3 asks the candidate to select the type of study or trial based on a description of what has actually been done.

Options

A   Cluster randomised trial
B   Long term follow up study
C   Meta-analysis
D   Non randomised 2 arm parallel group trial
E   Randomised 2 arm parallel group trial
F   Randomised crossover trial
G   Randomised factorial trial
H   Randomised multiple arm parallel group trial
I   Retrospective observational study
J   Short term follow up study
K   Single case study
L   Uncontrolled trial

Select the most appropriate type of trial from the list of options for each of the studies referred to in the items below. Each option may be used once, more than once or not at all.

ITEM 1

Women with pre-existing hypertension who then became pregnant volunteered for a study to compare a new antihypertensive drug taken orally with oral labetolol. Women were randomised to the new drug or labetolol and the 2 groups were followed up in order to study various clinical parameters. Both the women and the doctors who carried out the trial were deliberately kept unaware of which drug was being used in a certain woman.

ANSWER   E

ITEM 2

An expert committee studied the effect of umbilical artery Doppler analysis during pregnancy complicated by diabetes mellitus followed by appropriate management on the risk of stillbirth. A total of 25 studies

Thus far, the 2 questions which the candidate has answered in his/her mind have led to the correct answer. In the tragic case of the death of a live born baby, the candidate has to answer one question; what was the age of the baby in days at the time of death? In item 4 the baby dies at 6 days of age. Therefore, the answer is D.

In item 5 the baby dies at 12 days of age. The answer is E.

The definitions which pertain to loss of pregnancy are of fundamental importance and I would advise all candidates to memorise them. I would also wish to point out a pitfall which may trap the unwary candidate. A baby is delivered at a gestation of 21 weeks without any sign of life as in the scenario described in item 1. By definition, the woman has suffered a spontaneous miscarriage. Contrast this scenario where a woman suffers loss of pregnancy at 18 weeks gestation and the baby is born alive then dies. The classification of loss of pregnancy then depends on the age of the baby in days at the time of death. If the death of the baby is less than 7 completed days from the time of birth, the example is one of early neonatal death. If the death of the baby occurs after the seventh day but before 28 completed days from the time of birth then the example is one of late neonatal death. In this set of examples a woman who suffers loss of pregnancy at 21 weeks has, by definition, suffered a spontaneous miscarriage. However, a woman who has delivered a live baby at a much earlier stage in gestation which subsequently dies during the first week of life has suffered an early neonatal death. The woman has miscarried at 21 weeks would not be included in the perinatal statistics. The woman who has suffered loss of pregnancy at 18 weeks gestation leading to an early neonatal death would, perforce, be included in the perinatal statistics. Consider these points carefully. They are one of the keys you need to answer this type of EMQ.

E
M
Q

Now, let us look at some gynaecological EMQs. Again, the candidate may well be asked to interpret data. Consider worked example 5.

Options

A   4
B   0.4
C   0.44
D   0.044
E   0.0044
F   0.004
G   0.04
H   18
I   1.8
J   0.18

Large scale studies on the weight (in Kg) of healthy women at menarche were carried out and the weight of N women was measured reliably in each study. The weight of the women in each study showed a perfect Gaussian distribution. The list of options contains different values for standard error. Each of the items below provides a brief description of each study with the size of N, the mean and the standard deviation of the mean. Select the standard error in the study from the list of options. Each option may be used once, more than once or not at all.

ITEM 1
N=10,000. Mean=50 Kg. Standard deviation=4 Kg

ANSWER   G

The lead in statement describes a study and the results show a perfect Gaussian distribution. The candidate is advised that the list of options contains different values for standard error and is asked to calculate the standard error from the data provided in the item. How do you calculate standard error? The formula is a simple one to remember; standard error= standard deviation/$\sqrt{N}$.
In other words, divide standard deviation by the square root of the number of women in the study.
Let us read item 1. The information which you need; the value of

N and the standard deviation are provided. Why is the value of the mean also provided? In educational terms this is a "distractor". There will be distractors in the list of options; that is the very nature of EMQs. The wise candidate will ignore distractors in the items themselves.

Interpretation of endocrine profiles is a source of EMQs. The Examiners would provide different endocrine profiles in tabular form as in worked example 6.

Options

	Serum FSH	Serum LH	Serum Oestradiol	Serum Prolactin
A	Low	Low	Low	Low
B	Low	Low	Low	Normal
C	Elevated	Elevated	Low	Normal
D	Low	Low	Elevated	Elevated
E	Elevated	Elevated	Elevated	Elevated
F	Elevated	Low	Elevated	Undetectable
G	Low	Low	Elevated	Normal
H	Undetectable	Undetectable	Elevated	Elevated
I	Normal	Elevated	Normal	Normal
J	Normal	Normal	Normal	Elevated

The list of options shows the results of different endocrine tests. For each of the items below choose the profile that you would expect from the list of options. None of the women referred to in the items is taking any form of medication. Each option may be used once, more than once or not at all.

ITEM 1
A 40 year old woman with 6 living children delivered her seventh child vaginally and developed massive postpartum haemorrhage due to uterine atony. Although the woman was resuscitated she developed the clinical features of postpartum pituitary necrosis.

ANSWER A

ITEM 2

A woman underwent investigation of primary amenorrhoea. It was noted that she was of short stature and her karyotype was 45XO

ANSWER C

ITEM 3

A 36 year old woman underwent radiotherapy to the pelvis for Stage II invasive cancer of the cervix. Following treatment the woman complained of climacteric symptoms.

ANSWER C

There are several different profiles involving other hormones which could be used. This is one example. Generally, candidates are advised to read the lead in statement first. However, this is one example of an EMQ where a cursory glance at the headings on the table would be of assistance. Serum levels of FSH, LH, oestradiol and prolactin; the candidate is asked to identify the profiles which match the conditions described in the items. This EMQ can test knowledge of the inter relationship between isolated facts and more complex understanding. The validity of the test is enhanced as the scenarios bring the examination "right back to the clinic ".

Item 1 is an example of a woman suffering from Sheehan syndrome. Post partum pituitary necrosis lead to pituitary failure and serum FSH, LH and Prolactin levels are low. The ovaries were not stimulated and therefore the serum oestradiol was also low. The answer is A.

Ovarian failure can arise due to many conditions. The characteristic profile is elevated serum FSH and LH with a low serum oestradiol as the negative feedback effect of oestrogen on pituitary secretion of FSH and LH is lost.
In item 2 the ovaries are not functioning as the woman has Turner syndrome. The answer is C.
In item 3 the ovaries are not functioning as the pelvis has been irradiated. The answer is C.

Sometimes, some of the options in the list are highly implausible. These distractors are best ignored.

Consider worked example 7 which deals with genitourinary infection in non-pregnant women. The candidates' knowledge of the domain of diagnosis together with basic bench work is being tested.

Options

A   Bacterial vaginosis
B   Candidiasis
C   Chancroid
D   Chlamydial infection
E   Early syphilis
F   Gonorrhoea
G   Human papilloma virus infection
H   Leprosy
I   Leptospirosis
J   Schistosomiasis
K   Trichomoniasis
L   Tuberculosis

E
M
Q

The items below refer to non-pregnant women who attend clinic with clinical features of genital infection. You have taken an appropriate history, examined the woman and have the services of a reliable microbiology laboratory. Select the most likely diagnosis from the list of options. Each option may be used once, more than once or not at all.

ITEM 1

A 22 year old woman has a history of copious vaginal discharge and has tried several "over the counter" remedies to no effect. The woman's partner is a 22 year old man with a history of urethral discharge. On pelvic examination, there is a mucopurulent discharge on the cervix and an endocervical swab is taken. The material from the swab is stained with a certain fluorescein conjugated monoclonal antibody and viewed under an ultraviolet microscope. A large number of brightly coloured yellow-green dots appear.

ANSWER **D**

ITEM 2

A 30 year old woman complains of a malodorous vaginal discharge. On examination, there is a white vaginal discharge with vaginitis. Microscopic examination of material from a high vaginal swab shows the presence of clue cells. Her cervical smear shows the presence of mild dyskaryosis.

ANSWER A

ITEM 3

A 34 year old woman complained of vaginal discharge. On examination, there was a copious greyish coloured vaginal discharge. There was a "fishy" odour. The cervix appeared to be inflamed. Microscopic examination of material from a high vaginal swab showed the presence of actively motile flagellate protozoa.

ANSWER K

Item 1 describes the scenario of a woman whose male partner has non specific urethritis and she herself has a copious vaginal discharge. The presence of a mucopurulent cervical discharge is not diagnostic of anything. There is no mention of genital ulceration, vulval excoriation or warty growths. Thus far, the diagnostic possibilities become narrower. The material from the endocervical swab is examined under an ultraviolet microscope (rather than with background illumination and a light microscope) after staining with fluorescein conjugated monoclonal antibody. There is no mention of a Gram stain. By this stage, most candidates would have guessed the correct answer (as far as the test is concerned). The appearance of brightly coloured yellow-green dots (rather than coiled organisms or rods or cocci) points to Chlamydial infection. The bright yellow green dots which fix the monoclonal antibody (to Chlamydia) are elementary bodies. The answer is D

Why is mild dyskaryosis mentioned in the clinical scenario in item 2 of this EMQ? It is there as a distractor. The most likely answer is bacterial vaginosis whether or not the cervical smear is abnormal. The answer is A.

Item 3 is relatively straightforward. The woman has a malodorous vaginal discharge, the discharge is grey and copious and the cervix looks inflamed. Motile protozoa are identified in the material from the high vaginal swab. The protozoa are flagellate. Trichomonas vaginalis infection is being described. The answer is K.

Now for something more contentious. Consider worked example 8.

Options

A   Diagnostic
B   Excluded
C   Highly suspicious
D   Possible
E   Unlikely

E
M
Q

The list of options refers to the likelihood of a woman having cancer of the endometrium. For each of the items select the best description of the chance of cancer of the endometrium from the list of options. Each option may be used once, more than once or not at all.

ITEM 1

The woman is a 64 year old nullipara with a 4 week history of postmenopausal bleeding. The salient features on clinical examination are hypertension, body mass index of 36, blood in the vagina and a healthy cervix with a patulous os. Transvaginal ultrasound of the pelvis showed that the endometrial thickness was 3mm.

ANSWER   **C Highly suspicious**

ITEM 2

The woman is an otherwise healthy 52 year old multipara who had reached menopause one year ago. The woman started taking combined cyclical hormone replacement therapy for postmenopausal symptoms 4 weeks previously. Whilst on vacation, she took her medication irregularly and developed irregular vaginal bleeding for the last 2 weeks. The bleeding had stopped when she attended clinic, her body mass index was 21, there were no obvious abnormalities on examination and transvaginal ultrasound of the pelvis showed that the endometrial thickness was 1mm.

ANSWER   **E Unlikely**

ITEM 3

The woman is an otherwise healthy 52 year old multipara who started taking combined cyclical hormone replacement therapy for postmenopausal symptoms 2 years previously.

The medication was taken correctly and the woman developed slight and irregular vaginal bleeding for the last 2 weeks. The bleeding had stopped when she attended clinic, there were no obvious abnormalities on examination and transvaginal ultrasound of the pelvis showed that the endometrial thickness was 6mm.

ANSWER D Possible

ITEM 4

The woman is an otherwise healthy 52 year old multipara who complains of postmenopausal bleeding. The bleeding had stopped when she attended clinic, there were no obvious abnormalities on examination and transvaginal ultrasound of the pelvis showed that the endometrial thickness was 3mm. Hysteroscopy, with an excellent view showed the presence of inactive endometrium.

ANSWER B Excluded

Postmenopausal bleeding is due to endometrial cancer until proven otherwise. In order to pass the Part 2 MRCOG, candidates must demonstrate ability to reason on clinical grounds. Hence, the list of options contains different grades of certainty.

In item 1 the candidate is presented with the case of a 64 year old woman who is still bleeding from the cervical os at the time of examination. The item states that she has been bleeding for the last 4 weeks. There are other risk factors for endometrial cancer. On the other hand, there are guidelines which would state that an endometrial thickness of 3 mm or less indicates that no action needs to be taken in a woman who has never used hormone therapy. Back to item 1; there is no mention of hormone therapy. Puzzling? Need not be. The woman has postmenopausal bleeding; there are other risk factors and blood can be seen in the vagina. The endometrial thickness cannot be used as the basis for reassurance in this particular scenario. The answer is C.

In item 2 the answer is E. This is because the woman has only recently started hormone therapy; there is a plausible explanation for her symptoms and the endometrial thickness as measured by transvaginal ultrasound is 1 mm.

In item 3 the woman has been taking hormone therapy, has experienced unscheduled bleeding and the endometrial thickness is 6 mm. It is possible that the woman has endometrial cancer. The answer is D.

In item 4 the woman has undergone hysteroscopy with an excellent view. There is no evidence of endometrial cancer. The answer is B. This EMQ serves to illustrate an important point; some candidates may argue (reasonably) that a woman who has not used hormone therapy and who has an endometrial thickness of 3 mm or less need not undergo further tests unless there is a recurrence of symptoms. The point is that the EMQ requires candidates to select the risk of cancer of the endometrium and not to constructively criticise the management of the woman. I would reiterate the advice to read the lead-in statement, consider the items, ensure that you understand what is being asked and select the correct answer from the list of options. There is simply no need to attempt a rewrite of the EMQ or to do any more work than it requires.

E
M
Q

Key Points

1. Allow enough time for the EMQ section. Remember, there are 2 hours 45 minutes for the MCQ and EMQ papers which are now combined, with the College recommendation being to spend 90 minutes on the MCQs and 75 minutes on the EMQs. On a marks basis this slightly over weights the EMQs, although in practical terms most candidates find the MCQs easy to cover in less than 90 minutes and may well spend almost equal amounts of time on each paper. As the MCQs are worth 25% overall and the EMQs are worth only 15%, this is slightly misguided, although it is clear that EMQs are the greater challenge. I would suggest trimming the MCQ time to around 85 minutes and allowing 80 minutes for the EMQs. Therefore, aim to allow around 20 seconds for each separate MCQ item and two minutes for each EMQ item.

2. If you want to look at it from another angle, for each individual MCQ worth 1 mark, EMQs are worth 3.375 marks per item.

3. EMQs are designed to probe understanding and the ability to interpret.

4. Read the lead in statement first, then read the item(s), formulate the answer, select the answer from the list of options and mark the optical reader correctly.

There is a specimen EMQ paper with 40 items at the end of this book and the answers are provided. The items are different from those available in mrcogadvantage.com although some of the lists of options are similar.

The SAQs constitute 60% of the marks of the written paper. From an examination perspective, it is really worth tackling the SAQs and achieving high scores, although the "pass" mark for each SAQ will vary depending on the process of standard setting.

How much time is there for each SAQ in the Part 2 MRCOG examination? There are 26.25 minutes. Candidates must apportion their time carefully according to the marks allocated for each section of the SAQ.

Consider worked example 1.

A 24 year old woman has received standard antenatal care during her first pregnancy and just given birth to a male infant with a small open spina bifida at a gestation of 39 weeks. The lesion had not been detected before birth. Explain how you would counsel the woman (6 marks), write a risk assessment report (10 marks) and outline the management of her next pregnancy (4 marks).

A good candidate will cover the following;

Counselling;
- I would demonstrate my empathy, acknowledge that there is a critical incident, enquire about the baby's present condition and listen.
- The principles of counselling are to define, explore and clarify. In this context, I would establish exactly what the woman does and does not know about the condition of her baby.
- The relevant facts are that open neural tube defects arise with a frequency of about 1 in 500 in a North European or Indian population and that 90% of cases are detected by antenatal ultrasound.
- Ideally, all cases should be detected but 1 in 10 (approximately) are missed for various reasons including the small size of the defect and the position of the baby during the ultrasound examination. I would also clarify as to whether or not the woman did actually attend for the fetal morphology scan at the appropriate gestation.

- I would offer to show the woman local data on quality control and audit and arrange review of the images of the baby taken during antenatal ultrasound examination.
- I would arrange for the woman to be seen by the Paediatric services and acknowledge that surgery would be required and that physical handicap is an issue.

Marks 6

Risk assessment report;
- The essential features of the report must include why the critical incident occurred, whether appropriate systems were in place to prevent it and if so whether or not the relevant guidelines were followed.
- A key component of the report would include advice on how the risk of the incident happening again can be minimised.
- I would ensure that I sign, date and write my qualifications to carry out the risk assessment at the end of the report.
- I would arrange for statements to be collected from key care givers. In this particular case, statements from the staff that carried out the fetal anomaly scan are vital.
- Assessment of the recorded images from ultrasound examination. This is best carried out in a multidisciplinary meeting in a no blame culture.
- Details of antenatal care must be examined; the woman received standard care but exactly what does this mean? Was she seen by Midwives/Doctors of appropriate seniority? Was the woman referred for ultrasound examination at the appropriate stages during her pregnancy? What was the frequency of antenatal contact?
- Was the woman taking folic acid supplements prior to pregnancy?
- The report must examine whether or not the woman had clinical risk factors for fetal open neural tube defect which may not have been acted upon. Examples would include; maternal use of anticonvulsant medication, diabetes mellitus.
- The presence of antenatal clinical signs and whether they were recorded or managed appropriately would be a part of my report but this would be difficult to assess in retrospect. It would be useful to know whether polyhydramnios was ever suspected or actually recorded.

- Details of the birth; mode of delivery, birth weight and condition of the baby at birth. For example, the baby may be of low birth weight and small for dates as well.

Marks 10

Outline management of her next pregnancy;
- Preconceptual folic acid; 5 mg/day p.o. prior to conception.
- The woman should book under specialist care at an early stage of pregnancy.
- The woman must undergo antenatal ultrasound examination by 2 different scanners each of whom possess the appropriate qualifications and experience.
- The woman should be advised that amniocentesis for measurement of the alpha feto protein level in amniotic fluid is not necessary (if expert scanning is performed) in order to detect open neural tube defect and that the procedure carries a 1 % risk of fetal loss.

Marks 4

Commentary

A candidate will have 26.25 minutes to answer this. I would recommend that the SAQ is read twice before pen is put to paper. The purpose of the first reading is to grasp the meaning of the SAQ. Be sure that the words have been understood.

The purpose of the second reading is twofold; to identify and underline the key words and to understand the allocation of the marks. In worked example 1 it is clear that the opportunity for antenatal diagnosis of a serious fetal condition has been missed, there is the issue of breaking bad news, the woman must be counselled, a risk assessment report must be written and there is a need to make a few notes about the management of her next pregnancy. A second reading adds to the understanding of mark allocation. Half of the marks are allocated to the risk assessment report. A candidate would be unwise to focus on the other aspects of this SAQ to the detriment of the report. What about the key words? I would underline the following and add some notes as to their meaning and implication in the context of this SAQ;

Standard antenatal care; this woman underwent ultrasound examination

Just (given birth); the initial reaction would still be present
Small open spina bifida; bad enough
Lesion had not been detected before birth; issues of clinical governance and quality control
Counsel; define, explore, clarify
Risk assessment report; how and why an adverse event occurred and how it can be forestalled in the future
Outline; only a few minutes left.

The mark sheet provides an example of the detail which the Examiners would look for. A candidate should spend about 2 minutes planning the answer, approximately 7 or 8 minutes on the first part, 12 minutes on the second part and 4 minutes on the third part. I recommend writing in full sentences and forming paragraphs.

Consider worked example 2.

An otherwise healthy 38 year old woman with one living child complains of symptoms of premenstrual tension. How would you confirm the diagnosis (4 marks). What are the options for treatment (12 marks) and follow up (4 marks)?

A good candidate will cover the following;

Confirm the diagnosis;
- Diagnosis of PMT is based on the presence of cyclic symptoms which are physical, emotional and behavioural.
- Acknowledgement of the woman's problem is one of the most important steps
- Pelvic examination is very likely to be normal
- Details of relevance to treatment such as the woman's medical history, the age and wellbeing of her child and her feelings towards her own fertility must be ascertained.
Marks 4

Options for treatment;
- The woman's perception of the severity of her condition and its impact on her quality of life must be grasped. This influences options for treatment.
- In many women, a simple explanation of the condition and

reassurance that there is no physical disease may be sufficient.

reassurance that there is no physical disease may be sufficient.

- There is a rather high placebo effect of drug treatment
- Remedies include herbs, oils, combined ocp, pyridoxine, low dose oestrogen during the follicular phase
- The woman must be informed of the side effects of the medications she is using. Pyridoxine for example is a potential cause of neuropathy
- Some reports of success with paroxetine
- After simple remedies, consider GnRH analogue treatment, this is both a treatment and a diagnostic aid.
- The reduction of oestrogen levels would lead to a risk of osteoporosis
- Role of add back HRT. Even with HRT, the maximum recommended course of treatment is 6 months
- Must be emphasised to the woman that neither GnRH analogues or HRT are contraceptive in function
- Surgical intervention by bilateral salpingo-oophorectomy is a last resort
- Would need to consider long term oestrogen replacement therapy if the ovaries are resected.

Marks 12

Follow up after treatment;
- I would arrange follow up after any course of treatment in order to assess its effect if any. This includes side effects as well as therapeutic benefit.
- If GnRH analogue with HRT is being used I would review the woman after the first 3 injections, ensure that HRT is being used correctly and enquire as to whether or not the symptoms are coming under control. After this time amenorrhoea is likely.
- Once a course of medical treatment is finishes, the woman must be kept under regular review in order to assess any recurrence of symptoms. Further options for treatment may need to be explored.
- Following surgical removal of the ovaries, the woman would need to choose between oestrogen replacement therapy and other forms of prophylaxis against osteoporosis. Bone densitometry measurements would be advisable every 2 or 3 years.

Marks 4

Commentary

A comparatively straightforward SAQ which at first reading shows that the candidate is asked to write about premenstrual tension; its diagnosis, treatment and follow up. Options for treatment are allocated 12 out of 20 marks. The 2 other sections are allocated an equal 4 marks each. Clearly, the candidate must spend at least 13 minutes on options for treatment. The 2 other sections can be given approximately 5-6 minutes each.

The key words in this SAQ may be identified as follows;

Otherwise healthy 38 year old; the question is about what follows, not a lengthy differential diagnosis
Premenstrual tension; subject of the SAQ
How; the diagnosis of PMT is based on history taking
Diagnosis; a discussion on premenstrual tension will suffice
Options for treatment; there are many. Attempt to cover area and not just depth
Follow up; long term as well as medium term

Once candidates have written their answer, I would advise that approximately one minute is spent in checking for glaring mistakes in spelling and grammar.
Then, move on. It is tempting to spend more time in enhancing the answer. I would caution against this approach. It is unlikely that an afterthought would add more than one mark whereas many marks can be gained by going on to the next SAQ. It is vital that all SAQs are answered. I simply cannot overemphasise this point.

Key Points

1. Read the SAQ carefully twice; the first reading is to grasp its meaning.

2. Read the SAQ a second time in order to underline the key words and to understand the allocation of marks.

3. Plan the answer.

4. Allocate time in proportion to the marks allocated for each section.

5. Be specific in the answer.

6. Write clearly using sentences and paragraphs.

7. Check the answer.

8. Move on and complete the paper.

OSCEs

Excellent specimen OSCEs in DVD format may be obtained from Dalton Square Medical. "OSCES for the MRCOG Made Easy Volume 1 & 2" and are highly recommended.
I have written these two worked examples using data which form the basis for OSCEs in order to assist candidates for the Part 2 MRCOG examination.

Worked example 1 is an example of an OSCE with a role player. To illustrate and illuminate as much as possible, I have provided four forms - instructions to the candidate, instructions to the role player, instructions to the examiner and a sample of the mark sheet. Of course, all you will have in the oral assessment proper will be the first – instructions to the candidate, but will get the majority of the second (instructions to the role player) orally from the role player herself.

O
S
C
E

INSTRUCTIONS TO CANDIDATE

You are about to meet a 65 year old woman whose management so far has been less than ideal. The woman had been admitted under the duty surgical team 6 days previously with an "acute abdomen" and she underwent laparotomy under the care of the surgical team. The surgeons had found ascites, an ovarian tumour with "omental involvement" and multiple deposits in the pelvis. An ovarian biopsy was taken and the histopathological report shows that the ovarian tumour was an adenocarcinoma with spread to the omentum. The woman is rather introspective, remains an in-patient and is asking to see a doctor. You are asked to see her, explain the results of the report and plan further management. Your own consultant is away and the surgical team seems happy to transfer the woman's care.

You will be awarded marks for your ability to break bad news, answer the woman's questions and give appropriate advice.

- The CTG is reassuring, the results of the other tests are as follows;
  Serum Hb- 10.2 g/dl, WCC 11.5 ×109/l, platelets 84 × 109/l. serum urea 8.9 mmol/l,
  sodium 134 mmol/l, potassium 5.6 mmol/l,
  creatinine 110 mmol/l. Normal clotting profile.
- *What is your management?*
- Answer; stabilise with attention to prophylactic anticonvulsant, strict fluid balance and antihypertensive treatment.
  Anticonvulsive prophylaxis; I.V. Magnesium bolus followed by infusion.
  I.V fluids limited to 85 ml per hour, indwelling catheter to measure urine output, intake-output chart and nil by mouth.
  I.V.labetolol.
  Marks 4

- *What would be your choice of timing and mode of delivery?*
- Answer; Influenced by maternal and fetal condition. LSCS for urgent delivery especially if cervix is unfavourable, administration of steroids and waiting for 24 hours may well lead to a worse maternal and perinatal outcome. Need to inform anaesthetic and neonatal teams.
  Marks 4

- *Describe your plan of management for the first 12 hours following delivery*
- Answer; manage woman in a high dependency unit, continue plan of management in terms of fluid balance, I.V. Magnesium and I.V.labetolol, recheck clinical chemistry,
  Be aware of further complications.
  Marks 4

O
S
C
E

This is a straightforward structured oral test on an important Obstetric subject.

What are the learning points and what could go wrong?

INSTRUCTIONS TO CANDIDATE

The candidate is left in no doubt that knowledge of gestational proteinuric hypertension and the application of that knowledge to develop a safe and clear plan of management will gain marks. In the Part 2 MRCOG Examination, great care is taken to ensure that the candidate receives explicit instructions.

INSTRUCTIONS TO EXAMINER

Again, the guidance is explicit. In addition, there is advice that a maximum of 4 marks may be deducted for dangerous practice. If a candidate makes 3 or more factual errors the Examiner has the authority to deduct marks – one or two depending on the severity. In a worse case scenario six marks could thus be deducted – the lowest mark awarded is of course zero and not negative though. Thankfully, deductions are rare and should not worry well-prepared candidates at all. Avoid making wild or extravagant claims outside your knowledge.

MARK SHEET

The first 6 marks can be gained by answering a question on assessment. Candidates have already been informed that they will be tested on gestational proteinuric hypertension. What does "assessment" mean? It is the action of estimating or evaluating a condition. A 22 year old woman at 31 weeks into her first pregnancy with a hypertensive emergency, proteinuria and symptoms requires urgent assessment. What does initial mean? Existing or occurring at the beginning = initial. When the Examiner asks the candidate to describe" initial assessment", what is required is an expression of what the candidate would do first of all. The solution to any clinical problem starts with case history and physical examination then leads on to tests. The mark sheet serves as a guide to the Examiner. The specimen mark sheet provides examples of the type of information which the Examiner would expect. Candidates may get into errors of omission by ignoring the word "initial" and diving into ultrasound examination, CTG, blood tests and invasive haemodynamic monitoring. Again, the golden rule is to read the question carefully and to provide specific answers. Sometimes, the questions are easier than many candidates realise.

What investigations would you request? The risk at this stage is that candidates become focused on the maternal condition. How about the fetus? The question does not state that the baby is alive. It is possible that this woman's pregnancy has already been complicated by intrauterine fetal death. In the first section, it is important for the candidate to state that he/she would auscultate the fetal heart. A statement by the candidate that a CTG would be carried out in order to assess fetal wellbeing is required as part of the answer to the second section.

The next section on management is also straightforward. It is relevant to keep the woman "nil by mouth" as surgical intervention is likely. The key aspects of management of women with severe gestational proteinuric hypertension revolve around the following;

a) Management of fluid balance
b) Prophylaxis against eclampsia using i.v. magnesium sulphate
c) Anti-hypertensive treatment

Timing and mode of delivery are clearly determined by the maternal and fetal condition. Candidates must place themselves "in" the labour ward and tell the Examiner what they would do in these circumstances.

The final section deals with the immediate care of the woman after delivery. Candidates must demonstrate that they are fully aware of the life threatening conditions that may already be developing. It is worth remembering why women with gestational proteinuric hypertension may die;
Cerebro-vascular accident
Eclampsia
Cardiac failure
Adult respiratory distress syndrome
Acute renal failure
Acute liver failure
Disseminated intravascular coagulation

O
S
C
E

There may well be multi-organ failure. It is worth stating clearly that the woman must be cared for in a high dependency unit and not in the postnatal ward. This is another component of a safe and clear plan of management.

KEY POINTS

1. Read the question carefully. This is the golden rule.
2. Testing time is 14 minutes and this must be utilised fully.
3. Avoid hurrying and (equally) avoid being "stuck" in any one section. Remember that even in the OSCEs that are not clearly subdivided into sections, most OSCE marking sheets will indeed have several sections that need addressing.
4. Skills in interpersonal communication are vital.
5. Demonstrate the attitudes one would expect of a good Doctor.
6. Safety of the woman is a top priority.
7. Be pleasant and smile politely…even if you think that the test is not going well. It may be the opposite.
8. Do not feel intimidated by the Examiner's silence during a role player station. That is part of their instructions.

EMQ paper

Options

A Amniocentesis
B Chorionic villus sampling
C Counsel termination of pregnancy
D Determine carrier status of partner
E Obtain family records for linkage studies
F Reassure that there is no risk

Instructions: From the options above, select the **single** most appropriate next step in management for the woman in the clinical scenarios below.

1 A 28-year-old woman is 11 weeks into her first pregnancy and she is extremely concerned that her baby is affected by cystic fibrosis. The woman has two affected nephews both of whom are very ill and she has been identified as a gene carrier for cystic fibrosis.

Options

A Complete mole
B Diamniotic monochorionic twins
C Dizygotic twins
D Monoamniotic twins
E Monozygotic twinning with separate membranes and placentae
F Partial mole

Instructions: The list of options above refers to different results following fertilisation. Select the **single** most likely outcome for each of the scenarios in the items below. Each option may be used once, more than once or not at all.

2 Two separate oocytes produced during the same menstrual cycle are fertilised by two different spermatozoa.

3 The inner cell mass splits within the blastocyst.

Options

A   Breech can be palpated in the vagina but there is no descent after half an hour of maternal bearing down with contractions

B   Breech can be palpated in the vagina but there is no descent after one hour of maternal bearing down with contractions

C   Breech can be palpated in the vagina but there is no descent after two hours of maternal bearing down with contractions

D   Breech is in the sacro-lateral position and above level of the maternal ischial spines

E   Breech is in the sacro-lateral position and at the level of the maternal ischial spines

F   Breech is in the sacro-lateral position, below the level of the maternal ischial spines and the anterior buttock is seen at the introitus

G   Breech is in the sacro-lateral position, below the level of the maternal ischial spines and the posterior buttock is seen at the introitus

H   Breech is in the sacro-posterior position

I   Breech is outside the introitus

J   Breech is outside the introitus, the scapulae are seen and there is nuchal displacement of the fetal arms

K   Cervix is 9 cm dilated

L   Cervix is fully dilated

Instructions: An otherwise healthy 24-year-old multiparous woman with two living children (both of whom were delivered normally) is pregnant for the third time. The pregnancy has reached a gestational age of 39 weeks, there is a single fetus presenting by the breech and the woman has chosen to undergo vaginal breech delivery after the appropriate investigations and counselling. Labour has commenced spontaneously, there is an extended breech, progress in the first stage has been satisfactory and the intrapartum cardiotocogram has been reassuring. The list of options contains different findings during the conduct of vaginal breech delivery. Select the **single** most appropriate time for each of the actions in the items below. Each option may be used once, more than once or not at all.

4   Holding the breech using a femoro-pelvic grip

5   Lovset manoeuvre

Options

A   Avoid, but may be beneficial in some circumstances
B   Contraindicated
C   Contraindicated during third trimester only
D   Use without reservation

Instructions: For each of the vaccines in the items below select the most appropriate advice you would give to a pregnant woman from the list of options. Each option may be used once, more than once or not at all.

6   BCG

7   Diphtheria vaccine

8   Oral Typhoid vaccine

Options

A   Acute liver failure
B   Acute pancreatitis
C   Adult respiratory distress syndrome
D   Air embolism
E   Amniotic fluid embolism
F   Cerebellar tuberculosis
G   Cerebral tumour
H   Gestational proteinuric hypertension
I   Heamolytic uraemic syndrome
J   Massive intravascular haemolysis
K   Metastatic choriocarcinoma
L   Opiate poisoning
M   Pulmonary thromboembolism
N   Pulmonary tuberculosis
O   Subarachnoid haemorrhage
P   Thrombotic thrombocytopenic purpura

E
M
Q

Instructions: The list of options contains different causes of maternal mortality. Each of the scenarios itemised below refers to the death of a pregnant or puerperal woman. Select the **single** most likely cause of death from the list of options. Each option may be used once, more than once or not at all.

19 A 40-year-old woman was 41 weeks into her first pregnancy and she underwent induction of labour for post dates pregnancy using prostaglandin vaginal gel. Three hours after insertion of prostaglandin gel the woman appeared to be confused, breathless at rest and there was evidence of fetal distress in the cardiotocograph. On examination it was noted that her blood pressure was 100/45 mmHg, urine contained a significant amount of protein, serum Hb was 9.1 g/dl, white cell count was 20 × 109 per litre and the platelet count was 77 ×109 per litre. The cervix was 4 cm dilated, there was a single fetus presenting by the vertex in the occipito-anterior position and the amniotic fluid was stained with fresh meconium. Emergency lower segment caesarean section under general anaesthesia was carried out competently and a live infant was delivered in poor condition. The woman remained hypotensive postoperatively, developed tachypnoea and measurement of blood gases showed the presence of acidosis. Two hours following reversal of general anaesthesia, heavy vaginal bleeding occurred despite a well contracted uterus. Despite attempts at resuscitation the woman developed cardiac arrest and died. The main finding on post-mortem examination was the presence of material in the pulmonary vessels which stained positive with Alcian Blue dye.

20 An otherwise healthy 34-year-old pregnant woman was 30 weeks into her first pregnancy. The woman was performing vigorous exercise in the knee to chest position when she collapsed and died suddenly. Toxicological studies were negative and the main finding on post-mortem examination was the presence of dark frothy blood in the inferior vena cava, right atrium and right ventricle.

Options

A   Addison's disease
B   Androgen insensitivity syndrome
C   Kallman syndrome
D   Klinefelter syndrome
E   Mayer Rokitansky Kuster Hauser syndrome
F   Turner syndrome

Instructions: Each of the clinical scenarios below describes the development of a person who has primary amenorrhoea. Select the **single** most likely diagnosis from the list of options for each item. Each option may be used once, more than once or not at all.

21 The genotype is 46XX but there is deficient development of the Mullerian system. The uterus does develop but lacks a conduit to the vagina. Growth, ovarian function and development of the breasts are normal. Growth and appearance of pubic hair is consistent with a female phenotype. The serum testosterone is within the normal range for a female. Imaging shows that there is only one kidney.

22 The genotype is 46XY. The presence of anti Mullerian hormone leads to an absence of the Fallopian tubes, uterus and upper vagina. There is no response to androgens and critical steps in male sexual differentiation fail to take place. Growth and development of the breasts are normal. The serum testosterone is within the normal range for a male. Urinary excretion of 17 keto steroids is within the normal range.

Options

A 2 µg
B 20 µg
C 200 µg
D 800 µg
E 2 mg
F 20 mg
G 200 mg
H 2 g
I 8 g
J 10 g

23 The levonorgestrel coated intrauterine system releases a certain amount of levonorgestrel into the uterus. Select the mass of levonorgestrel from the list of options above which most closely matches the amount which is released over 24 hours.

Options

A 500
B 100
C 25
D 5
E 0.5
F 0.05
G 0.005
H 0.0005

Instructions: Large scale studies on the weight (in kg) of healthy women at menarche were carried out and the weight of N women was measured reliably in each study. The weight of the women in each study showed a perfect Gaussian distribution. The list of options contains different values for standard error. The item below provides a brief description of a study including the size of N and the value of the mean. Select the standard error in the study from the list of options.

24 In this study, the value of N was 10,000, the mean weight was 50 kg and 6,800 women had a weight between 45 kg and 55 kg.

E
M
Q

Options

A   Cardinal ligament
B   Fallopian tube with cardinal ligament
C   Fallopian tube with ovarian ligament
D   Fallopian tube with urachus
E   Infundibulopelvic ligament
F   Ligamentum teres
G   Round ligament
H   Uterosacral ligament

Instructions: During the course of the operation of abdominal total hysterectomy, certain pedicles must be clamped, divided and ligatured. In each of the scenarios below, the woman has undergone laparotomy and is about to undergo abdominal total hysterectomy for dysfunctional uterine bleeding. The Surgeon has clamped the round ligament, ovarian ligament and Fallopian tube at their connection to the uterus. The list of options contains different anatomical structures. For the item below, select the option which best describes which structure(s) must be clamped, divided and ligatured as the next step in the operation.

25 The surgeon intends to conserve the ovaries

Options

A   Benign intra-epidermal cyst
B   Granular cell tumour
C   Granuloma inguinale
D   Herpetic vulivtis
E   Lichen sclerosus
F   Malignant melanoma
G   Primary syphilis
H   Secondary syphilis

Instructions: Select the **single** most closely matching diagnosis from the list of options above for the scenario and histopathological findings which are described in the item below.

26 A 10-year-old girl complained of vulval soreness and pain on defaecation. The salient feature on examination was a 'dumbbell' shaped rash which involved the skin around the vulva and anus. The lesion consisted of white atrophic patches with a few red spots. A vulval biopsy was taken under local anaesthesia. Histological examination showed hyperkeratosis, thinning of the epidermis and flattening of the rete ridges. There was oedema in the superficial dermis and hyalinised connective tissue. Below the dermis, there was mild chronic inflammation.

E
M
Q

Options

A   Attrition
B   Measurement
C   Performance
D   Publication
E   Selection

Instructions: Bias either exaggerates or underestimates the true effect of an intervention or exposure. The list of options contains different types of bias. The items below describe different prospective studies in which two different groups of postmenopausal women were compared in order to study the relationship between breast cancer and the use of hormone replacement therapy. One group received a currently available combined preparation (group A) and the other group received a new preparation which contained a new progesterone but the same oestrogen (group B). Select the **single** most significant type of bias in each item from the list of options. Each option may be used once, more than once or not at all.

27 The women were randomly allocated into the two groups and the health care providers and women themselves were "blinded" as to which group they were in. Objective measures were used to measure the incidence of breast cancer in the two groups. Exactly the same measures were used in each group. Almost 60% of the participants in group B dropped out of the study.

28 The women were randomly allocated into the two groups and the health care providers and women themselves were 'blinded' as to which group they were in. Objective measures were used to measure the incidence of breast cancer in the two groups. There were no differences in the drop out rate between the two groups. Objective measures were used to measure the incidence of breast cancer in the two groups and exactly the same measures were used in each group. The statistical tests which were used had adequate power. The study showed that there was no difference between the two groups in terms of the incidence of breast cancer ten years later. The researchers wrote a paper which was turned down for publication in three peer reviewed journals.

Options

A   Benign cystic teratoma
B   Cervical adenocarcinoma
C   Choriocarcinoma
D   Dysgerminoma
E   Endometrial carcinoma
F   Fibroid
G   Mixed Mullerian tumour
H   Uterine sarcoma
I   Sarcoma botryoides
J   Yolk sac tumour

Instructions: Select the **single** most closely matching tumour from the list of options for each scenario in the items below. Each option may be used once, more than once or not at all.

29 A 75-year-old woman had a rapidly enlarging pelvic mass and postmenopausal bleeding. Following the appropriate investigations and counselling the woman underwent total abdominal hysterectomy and bilateral salpingo-oophorectomy. Gross examination of the specimen showed that the uterus was enlarged and the ovaries were small. There was a soft polypoidal tumour mass filling the enlarged uterine cavity.

30 A 34-year-old Chinese woman with three living children underwent suction evacuation of the uterus for molar pregnancy at a gestation of 12 weeks. The woman was monitored appropriately and her serum β-HCG rose sharply over three weeks following the operation. Then, the woman was readmitted with very heavy vaginal bleeding and required emergency abdominal hysterectomy. Gross examination of the uterus showed that it was bulky and soft. There was a haemorrhagic, cystic, blackish brown tumour within the uterine cavity.

31 A 22-year-old nulliparous woman was admitted through the emergency department with abdominal pain. Clinical assessment showed the presence of a pelvic mass and ultrasound examination demonstrated that the lesion was a solid ovarian tumour. The woman underwent laparotomy and right salpingo-oophorectomy under the care of the oncology team. It was noted that the left ovary was normal. Examination of the operation specimen showed that there was a capsule and the lesion was a monomorphic solid. On cutting into the specimen, its consistency was that of a potato and the cut surface was fleshy.

Options

	Type	Toxicity
A	Alkylating agent	Cardiotoxic
B	Alkylating agent	Myelotoxic. Cystitis
C	Alkylating agent	Ototoxic
D	Alkylating agent	Pulmonary fibrosis
E	Antibiotic	Cystitis
F	Antibiotic	Hepatotoxic
G	Antibiotic	Myelotoxic
H	Antibiotic	Myelotoxic. Cardiotoxic
I	Antibiotic	Pneumonitis. Hyperpigmentation of the skin
J	Antibiotic	Toxic to cranial nerves
K	Antimetabolite	Myelotoxic
L	Antimetabolite	Myelotoxic .Ototoxic. Cardiotoxic
M	Antimetabolite	Nephrotoxic
N	Antimetabolite	Skin pigmentation
O	Plant alkaloid	Cortical blindness
P	Plant alkaloid	Metabolic alkalosis
Q	Plant alkaloid	Myelotoxic
R	Plant alkaloid	Myelotoxic. Neurotoxic
S	Plant alkaloid	Myelotoxic. Occasionally Cardiotoxic
T	Plant alkaloid	Nephrotoxic. Myelotoxic

Instructions: The list of options refers to types of cytotoxic drugs used in chemotherapy and toxicities. Select the **single** appropriate option which describes the type of drug and characteristic toxicity for each of the drugs in the items below. Each option may be used once, more than once or not at all.

32 Cyclophosphamide

33 Gemcitabine

34 Bleomycin

Options

A   Cancel the operation
B   Consider an alternative pharmacological intervention
C   Defer for one month
D   Defer for one week
E   Defer operation and discuss at a multidisciplinary oncology case conference
F   Discuss management with the woman's family
G   Proceed on an emergency basis
H   Proceed with the operation as planned

Instructions: The items below refer to women who have been scheduled to undergo gynaecological surgery for various reasons. However, you asked to review the timing of the operation in view of new clinical information. Choose the **single** most appropriate management from the list of options. Each option may be used once, more than once or not at all.

35   An otherwise healthy 28-year-old woman is scheduled to undergo diagnostic laparoscopy for pelvic pain. The woman had been waiting to undergo the operation for the last 10 weeks. You are asked to see her on the morning of the scheduled operation as the admitting doctor identified a small area of resolving cellulitis around the umbilicus without any discharge. The woman had removed a small piece of body jewellery from her umbilicus four days previously.

36   A 40 year old woman has been admitted with the features of a ruptured ectopic pregnancy. Her blood pressure is 65/40 mmHg, pulse rate 120/min, cold peripheries and the serum Hb is 8.2 g/dl. The junior anaesthetist queries the urgency of the operation and you are asked for a decision.

Options

A   Anorexia nervosa
B   Panic disorder
C   Personality disorder
D   Premenstrual syndrome
E   Psychotic illness
F   Reactive depression

Instructions: Each item below refers to a woman with a four-month history of the symptoms being described. In each case the woman has a regular cycle and the results of pelvic examination and serum endocrine profile are normal. Select the **single** most likely cause for the woman's symptoms from the list of options. Each option may be used once, more than once or not at all.

37 The woman is aged 38 years, she has been pregnant once and she has a healthy two year old child. The woman reports a feeling of "being low" all the time, a tendency to react angrily to her partner and insomnia. Four months previously the woman had suffered bereavement and feels that her low affect may have started from that time. The woman describes her partner as "a very patient, nice guy" and she is worried that her changes are affecting their relationship. The woman works as a cleaner in the local hospice but has considered stopping as she feels unable to concentrate at work, feels tired all the time and received a disciplinary warning from her employer. The symptoms do not appear to have any relationship to menstruation.

38 The woman is aged 28 years, she has been pregnant once and she has a healthy two year old child. Despite her career as a successful lawyer the woman has experienced thoughts of self-deprecation and a sense of hopelessness. The woman's husband has noticed that she feels very "keyed up" and also reports that she has unusually marked emotional lability. The couple report that the symptoms are worse during the week before menstruation when there is occasional insomnia (in addition to the other symptoms) and a tendency to consume large amounts of chocolate. The symptoms disappear almost completely within a few days of the onset of menstruation.

Options

A   Deficit = £1,250
B   Deficit = £12,500
C   Deficit = £35,000
D   Deficit = £45,000
E   Deficit = £45,500
F   Deficit = £67,500
G   Deficit = £135,000
H   Surplus = £100
I   Surplus = £1,000
J   Surplus = £5,000
K   Surplus = £10,000
L   Surplus = £20,000
M   Surplus = £50,000
N   Surplus = £80,000
O   Surplus = £90,000

Instructions: Your Department is given a budget of £100,000 solely for the purchase of a drug which is used to treat overactive bladder. The budget has to cover the cost of dispensing two different doses of the drug over one year for all the women who need treatment. There are 900 women who need the drug. The cost per woman is £100 per year if the low dose is used and £150 per year if the high dose of the drug is used. The list of options contains different outcomes for the budget. For each of the scenarios below choose the single correct option. Each option may be used once, more than once or not at all.

39 800 women use the low dose drug with good effect and 100 women use the high dose of the drug over the year.

40 All the women need the high dose preparation for the whole year.

EMQ Answer Paper

1	[A]	[B]	[C]	[D]	[E]	[F]	[G]	[H]	[I]	[J]	[K]	[L]	[M]	[N]	[O]	[P]	[Q]	[R]	[S]	[T]
2	[A]	[B]	[C]	[D]	[E]	[F]	[G]	[H]	[I]	[J]	[K]	[L]	[M]	[N]	[O]	[P]	[Q]	[R]	[S]	[T]
3	[A]	[B]	[C]	[D]	[E]	[F]	[G]	[H]	[I]	[J]	[K]	[L]	[M]	[N]	[O]	[P]	[Q]	[R]	[S]	[T]
4	[A]	[B]	[C]	[D]	[E]	[F]	[G]	[H]	[I]	[J]	[K]	[L]	[M]	[N]	[O]	[P]	[Q]	[R]	[S]	[T]
5	[A]	[B]	[C]	[D]	[E]	[F]	[G]	[H]	[I]	[J]	[K]	[L]	[M]	[N]	[O]	[P]	[Q]	[R]	[S]	[T]
6	[A]	[B]	[C]	[D]	[E]	[F]	[G]	[H]	[I]	[J]	[K]	[L]	[M]	[N]	[O]	[P]	[Q]	[R]	[S]	[T]
7	[A]	[B]	[C]	[D]	[E]	[F]	[G]	[H]	[I]	[J]	[K]	[L]	[M]	[N]	[O]	[P]	[Q]	[R]	[S]	[T]
8	[A]	[B]	[C]	[D]	[E]	[F]	[G]	[H]	[I]	[J]	[K]	[L]	[M]	[N]	[O]	[P]	[Q]	[R]	[S]	[T]
9	[A]	[B]	[C]	[D]	[E]	[F]	[G]	[H]	[I]	[J]	[K]	[L]	[M]	[N]	[O]	[P]	[Q]	[R]	[S]	[T]
10	[A]	[B]	[C]	[D]	[E]	[F]	[G]	[H]	[I]	[J]	[K]	[L]	[M]	[N]	[O]	[P]	[Q]	[R]	[S]	[T]
11	[A]	[B]	[C]	[D]	[E]	[F]	[G]	[H]	[I]	[J]	[K]	[L]	[M]	[N]	[O]	[P]	[Q]	[R]	[S]	[T]
12	[A]	[B]	[C]	[D]	[E]	[F]	[G]	[H]	[I]	[J]	[K]	[L]	[M]	[N]	[O]	[P]	[Q]	[R]	[S]	[T]
13	[A]	[B]	[C]	[D]	[E]	[F]	[G]	[H]	[I]	[J]	[K]	[L]	[M]	[N]	[O]	[P]	[Q]	[R]	[S]	[T]
14	[A]	[B]	[C]	[D]	[E]	[F]	[G]	[H]	[I]	[J]	[K]	[L]	[M]	[N]	[O]	[P]	[Q]	[R]	[S]	[T]
15	[A]	[B]	[C]	[D]	[E]	[F]	[G]	[H]	[I]	[J]	[K]	[L]	[M]	[N]	[O]	[P]	[Q]	[R]	[S]	[T]
16	[A]	[B]	[C]	[D]	[E]	[F]	[G]	[H]	[I]	[J]	[K]	[L]	[M]	[N]	[O]	[P]	[Q]	[R]	[S]	[T]
17	[A]	[B]	[C]	[D]	[E]	[F]	[G]	[H]	[I]	[J]	[K]	[L]	[M]	[N]	[O]	[P]	[Q]	[R]	[S]	[T]
18	[A]	[B]	[C]	[D]	[E]	[F]	[G]	[H]	[I]	[J]	[K]	[L]	[M]	[N]	[O]	[P]	[Q]	[R]	[S]	[T]
19	[A]	[B]	[C]	[D]	[E]	[F]	[G]	[H]	[I]	[J]	[K]	[L]	[M]	[N]	[O]	[P]	[Q]	[R]	[S]	[T]
20	[A]	[B]	[C]	[D]	[E]	[F]	[G]	[H]	[I]	[J]	[K]	[L]	[M]	[N]	[O]	[P]	[Q]	[R]	[S]	[T]
21	[A]	[B]	[C]	[D]	[E]	[F]	[G]	[H]	[I]	[J]	[K]	[L]	[M]	[N]	[O]	[P]	[Q]	[R]	[S]	[T]
22	[A]	[B]	[C]	[D]	[E]	[F]	[G]	[H]	[I]	[J]	[K]	[L]	[M]	[N]	[O]	[P]	[Q]	[R]	[S]	[T]
23	[A]	[B]	[C]	[D]	[E]	[F]	[G]	[H]	[I]	[J]	[K]	[L]	[M]	[N]	[O]	[P]	[Q]	[R]	[S]	[T]
24	[A]	[B]	[C]	[D]	[E]	[F]	[G]	[H]	[I]	[J]	[K]	[L]	[M]	[N]	[O]	[P]	[Q]	[R]	[S]	[T]
25	[A]	[B]	[C]	[D]	[E]	[F]	[G]	[H]	[I]	[J]	[K]	[L]	[M]	[N]	[O]	[P]	[Q]	[R]	[S]	[T]
26	[A]	[B]	[C]	[D]	[E]	[F]	[G]	[H]	[I]	[J]	[K]	[L]	[M]	[N]	[O]	[P]	[Q]	[R]	[S]	[T]
27	[A]	[B]	[C]	[D]	[E]	[F]	[G]	[H]	[I]	[J]	[K]	[L]	[M]	[N]	[O]	[P]	[Q]	[R]	[S]	[T]
28	[A]	[B]	[C]	[D]	[E]	[F]	[G]	[H]	[I]	[J]	[K]	[L]	[M]	[N]	[O]	[P]	[Q]	[R]	[S]	[T]
29	[A]	[B]	[C]	[D]	[E]	[F]	[G]	[H]	[I]	[J]	[K]	[L]	[M]	[N]	[O]	[P]	[Q]	[R]	[S]	[T]
30	[A]	[B]	[C]	[D]	[E]	[F]	[G]	[H]	[I]	[J]	[K]	[L]	[M]	[N]	[O]	[P]	[Q]	[R]	[S]	[T]
31	[A]	[B]	[C]	[D]	[E]	[F]	[G]	[H]	[I]	[J]	[K]	[L]	[M]	[N]	[O]	[P]	[Q]	[R]	[S]	[T]
32	[A]	[B]	[C]	[D]	[E]	[F]	[G]	[H]	[I]	[J]	[K]	[L]	[M]	[N]	[O]	[P]	[Q]	[R]	[S]	[T]
33	[A]	[B]	[C]	[D]	[E]	[F]	[G]	[H]	[I]	[J]	[K]	[L]	[M]	[N]	[O]	[P]	[Q]	[R]	[S]	[T]
34	[A]	[B]	[C]	[D]	[E]	[F]	[G]	[H]	[I]	[J]	[K]	[L]	[M]	[N]	[O]	[P]	[Q]	[R]	[S]	[T]
35	[A]	[B]	[C]	[D]	[E]	[F]	[G]	[H]	[I]	[J]	[K]	[L]	[M]	[N]	[O]	[P]	[Q]	[R]	[S]	[T]
36	[A]	[B]	[C]	[D]	[E]	[F]	[G]	[H]	[I]	[J]	[K]	[L]	[M]	[N]	[O]	[P]	[Q]	[R]	[S]	[T]
37	[A]	[B]	[C]	[D]	[E]	[F]	[G]	[H]	[I]	[J]	[K]	[L]	[M]	[N]	[O]	[P]	[Q]	[R]	[S]	[T]
38	[A]	[B]	[C]	[D]	[E]	[F]	[G]	[H]	[I]	[J]	[K]	[L]	[M]	[N]	[O]	[P]	[Q]	[R]	[S]	[T]
39	[A]	[B]	[C]	[D]	[E]	[F]	[G]	[H]	[I]	[J]	[K]	[L]	[M]	[N]	[O]	[P]	[Q]	[R]	[S]	[T]
40	[A]	[B]	[C]	[D]	[E]	[F]	[G]	[H]	[I]	[J]	[K]	[L]	[M]	[N]	[O]	[P]	[Q]	[R]	[S]	[T]

EMQ paper answer key

1 [A] [B] [C] **[D]** [E] [F] [G] [H] [I] [J] [K] [L] [M] [N] [O] [P] [Q] [R] [S] [T]
2 [A] [B] **[C]** [D] [E] [F] [G] [H] [I] [J] [K] [L] [M] [N] [O] [P] [Q] [R] [S] [T]
3 [A] **[B]** [C] [D] [E] [F] [G] [H] [I] [J] [K] [L] [M] [N] [O] [P] [Q] [R] [S] [T]
4 [A] [B] [C] [D] [E] [F] [G] [H] **[I]** [J] [K] [L] [M] [N] [O] [P] [Q] [R] [S] [T]
5 [A] [B] [C] [D] [E] [F] [G] [H] [I] **[J]** [K] [L] [M] [N] [O] [P] [Q] [R] [S] [T]
6 [A] **[B]** [C] [D] [E] [F] [G] [H] [I] [J] [K] [L] [M] [N] [O] [P] [Q] [R] [S] [T]
7 **[A]** [B] [C] [D] [E] [F] [G] [H] [I] [J] [K] [L] [M] [N] [O] [P] [Q] [R] [S] [T]
8 [A] **[B]** [C] [D] [E] [F] [G] [H] [I] [J] [K] [L] [M] [N] [O] [P] [Q] [R] [S] [T]
9 [A] [B] [C] **[D]** [E] [F] [G] [H] [I] [J] [K] [L] [M] [N] [O] [P] [Q] [R] [S] [T]
10 [A] **[B]** [C] [D] [E] [F] [G] [H] [I] [J] [K] [L] [M] [N] [O] [P] [Q] [R] [S] [T]
11 [A] [B] [C] [D] **[E]** [F] [G] [H] [I] [J] [K] [L] [M] [N] [O] [P] [Q] [R] [S] [T]
12 [A] [B] [C] [D] [E] **[F]** [G] [H] [I] [J] [K] [L] [M] [N] [O] [P] [Q] [R] [S] [T]
13 [A] [B] **[C]** [D] [E] [F] [G] [H] [I] [J] [K] [L] [M] [N] [O] [P] [Q] [R] [S] [T]
14 [A] [B] [C] [D] [E] [F] [G] [H] **[I]** [J] [K] [L] [M] [N] [O] [P] [Q] [R] [S] [T]
15 [A] [B] [C] [D] [E] [F] [G] [H] [I] **[J]** [K] [L] [M] [N] [O] [P] [Q] [R] [S] [T]
16 [A] [B] [C] [D] [E] [F] [G] [H] [I] **[J]** [K] [L] [M] [N] [O] [P] [Q] [R] [S] [T]
17 [A] [B] [C] [D] [E] [F] [G] **[H]** [I] [J] [K] [L] [M] [N] [O] [P] [Q] [R] [S] [T]
18 [A] [B] [C] [D] **[E]** [F] [G] [H] [I] [J] [K] [L] [M] [N] [O] [P] [Q] [R] [S] [T]
19 [A] [B] [C] [D] **[E]** [F] [G] [H] [I] [J] [K] [L] [M] [N] [O] [P] [Q] [R] [S] [T]
20 [A] [B] [C] **[D]** [E] [F] [G] [H] [I] [J] [K] [L] [M] [N] [O] [P] [Q] [R] [S] [T]
21 [A] [B] [C] [D] **[E]** [F] [G] [H] [I] [J] [K] [L] [M] [N] [O] [P] [Q] [R] [S] [T]
22 [A] **[B]** [C] [D] [E] [F] [G] [H] [I] [J] [K] [L] [M] [N] [O] [P] [Q] [R] [S] [T]
23 [A] **[B]** [C] [D] [E] [F] [G] [H] [I] [J] [K] [L] [M] [N] [O] [P] [Q] [R] [S] [T]
24 [A] [B] [C] [D] [E] **[F]** [G] [H] [I] [J] [K] [L] [M] [N] [O] [P] [Q] [R] [S] [T]
25 [A] [B] **[C]** [D] [E] [F] [G] [H] [I] [J] [K] [L] [M] [N] [O] [P] [Q] [R] [S] [T]
26 [A] [B] [C] [D] **[E]** [F] [G] [H] [I] [J] [K] [L] [M] [N] [O] [P] [Q] [R] [S] [T]
27 **[A]** [B] [C] [D] [E] [F] [G] [H] [I] [J] [K] [L] [M] [N] [O] [P] [Q] [R] [S] [T]
28 [A] [B] [C] **[D]** [E] [F] [G] [H] [I] [J] [K] [L] [M] [N] [O] [P] [Q] [R] [S] [T]
29 [A] [B] [C] [D] [E] [F] **[G]** [H] [I] [J] [K] [L] [M] [N] [O] [P] [Q] [R] [S] [T]
30 [A] [B] **[C]** [D] [E] [F] [G] [H] [I] [J] [K] [L] [M] [N] [O] [P] [Q] [R] [S] [T]
31 [A] [B] [C] **[D]** [E] [F] [G] [H] [I] [J] [K] [L] [M] [N] [O] [P] [Q] [R] [S] [T]
32 [A] **[B]** [C] [D] [E] [F] [G] [H] [I] [J] [K] [L] [M] [N] [O] [P] [Q] [R] [S] [T]
33 [A] [B] [C] [D] [E] [F] [G] [H] [I] [J] **[K]** [L] [M] [N] [O] [P] [Q] [R] [S] [T]
34 [A] [B] [C] [D] [E] [F] [G] [H] **[I]** [J] [K] [L] [M] [N] [O] [P] [Q] [R] [S] [T]
35 [A] [B] [C] **[D]** [E] [F] [G] [H] [I] [J] [K] [L] [M] [N] [O] [P] [Q] [R] [S] [T]
36 [A] [B] [C] [D] [E] [F] **[G]** [H] [I] [J] [K] [L] [M] [N] [O] [P] [Q] [R] [S] [T]
37 [A] [B] [C] [D] [E] **[F]** [G] [H] [I] [J] [K] [L] [M] [N] [O] [P] [Q] [R] [S] [T]
38 [A] [B] [C] **[D]** [E] [F] [G] [H] [I] [J] [K] [L] [M] [N] [O] [P] [Q] [R] [S] [T]
39 [A] [B] [C] [D] [E] [F] [G] [H] [I] **[J]** [K] [L] [M] [N] [O] [P] [Q] [R] [S] [T]
40 [A] [B] **[C]** [D] [E] [F] [G] [H] [I] [J] [K] [L] [M] [N] [O] [P] [Q] [R] [S] [T]